Queen, Get your MoJo back

CONQUERING LOSS OF IDENTITY IN MOTHERHOOD

NOELLE MAPIANDA

NOELLE MAPIANDA
Copyright © 2022 Noelle Mapianda
All rights reserved.
ISBN: 9798835775699 (paperback)

Dedication

I am grateful to God for the privilege to be in the land of the living and for the ability to write.

I would like to dedicate **Queen, Get your Mojo Back** to all the women in the world, especially the working mothers.

To my husband Medyt Pika and gorgeous daughter Shalom Pika, I love you dearly. You are my inspiration!

Table of Contents

Dedicated   iii
Preface   vii
Introduction   xiii

History   1
Childbirth   9
Change   13
Exposure   17
Loss of Identity in Motherhood   22
Research   25
Is Self Identity A Cultural Issue?   51
How Did Previous Generation Cope With Identity Loss?   56
My Personal Experience   57
In Hindsight   70
Why is Motherhood Important?   72
Finance   76

Conclusion   81
Final Words   85
Acknowlegements   89
References   91

Preface

Self-identity is a vital conversation to be had in our society today. I've had a series of such conversations with myself about it, especially since becoming a mother. I've also had similar conversations with other women in my position. I've discovered we have a lot in common. We are professionals and mothers. We all felt like we had lost our sense of self-identity at some point when becoming mothers. The dual nature of the role created a sense of imbalance in our lives. We had to face pressures from our professions as well as the ones in our homes.

As soon as I hit my thirties, I wanted to start a family. At the same time, I was very ambitious and wanted to advance my career. As my journey progressed, I found that although it wasn't an impossible task, emotionally it was draining. At times I found it very difficult to balance life in general and motherhood. While on maternity leave reality finally caught up and I sensed I was losing a part of me. My focus was shifting and I was becoming someone I didn't recognise or necessarily want to be.

I come from a family of five. I never saw my mother take a career break. Her career and motherhood ran in parallel. She played both roles as it was expected of her, at least in her culture. As a young girl, this is the image I had painted for myself. I knew that at some point, I would also become a mother and pursue my career like my mother did. My time came, I became a mother and at the same time I was trying to hold on to my career. I suddenly realised that my expectations and reality were different. I didn't take into account the fact my mother had me in a completely different environment and culture. In my culture, a child is raised by the community, the entire village. I live in England and things are completely different. This created a lot of clash in my mind.

During one encounter, I was asked by someone: "how will you define your identity?". It took me by surprise to be honest but after sometimes, I came up with an answer. I basically said that I am *a medley of identities*. I am a wife, a mother, a woman of colour, a professional, an academic and a woman of faith. As such I feel like I have several facets to my self-identity. It is almost like wearing a veil, which comes on and off depending on the context. Every identity I possess has a vital role to play in my life. I am what I am because of those traits. I am the merged version of all my identities. This then, convinces me that I have never lost my identity in motherhood but rather I discovered another part of myself which was yet to be explored. You see, giving birth to my daughter is also an extension of me, since she came from me.

Motherhood is a new added layer to my identity that I will call the *motherly gene*. I can say that any conflict I have encountered during my transition from womanhood to motherhood can only be attributed to the fact that it was a new territory, a new experience. This makes me think about how our immune system operates. Whenever it senses a foreign entity, scientifically known as an antigen, it works hard to recognise it and gets rid of it. The immune system is comprised of two parts. The first is the innate immune system, which we are born with it. The second is the adaptive immune system. Both the innate and adaptive immune systems primarily role is to protect us against invaders. But, the adaptive immune system goes further as it produces antibodies. These in turn, not only defend the body but they also keep record of the attack so that when the body is exposed to a similar invader again, its response will be much faster.

We can say that there is rivalry between our precedent self-identity and the acquired one from motherhood. The old self wants to dominate and suppress the new. But, once we can master them both, they can work to our advantage and cooperate like the innate and adaptive human systems do.

What then is identity?

According to the Merriam-Webster online dictionary:

Identity is defined as follows:

The distinguishing character or personality of an individual: individuality.

Or the relation established by psychological identification.

I've mentioned earlier that I consider myself a medley of identities. I am one individual with several identities. These showcase themselves when needed, depending on the context. There are times where my identities are used interchangeably. Based on this, I wanted to discuss other types of identity we can relate with.

The first one is familial identity: this is when we are socially conditioned by our environment and upbringing from the people around us, our family and community since childhood. This in turn shapes our values and beliefs system, the way we view the world around us. For example, I am a woman of colour of an African descent, with that, I was brought up in a different environment. As a young girl, I was expected to be able to look after our household as an adult would. I was made responsible from a very younger age. Sadly, this could be considered indicative of those cultural stereotypes, where women are expected to be good at house chores.

The second is associative identity: as the name suggests – this is when we identify with our associations. This could include our racial identity, ancestry or physical appearance. This would influence our sense of fashion style, our music preferences, the people we spend the time with or our political affiliations. For example, most of my black women friends at some point opted for natural hair. We all used to relax our hair. If you don't know, hair relaxing is using chemicals to straighten the hair. Recently, there have been discussions about and the growth in movements where black women are identifying more with their natural hair. I have joined the clan.

The third one is Ego identity: this is instinctual protective identity as it provides us with a very strong sense of self. It emphasises the sense of who we are and causes us to also act on that sense in a way that is consistent and coherent. For example, when someone has a very dominant character, they are noticed whenever they enter a room.

The fourth one is existential identity: this can be defined as the way we view ourselves or the identity we attribute to ourselves as individuals. An identity we ultimately choose to exist in. For example, when an athlete or a sports person receives a career-curtailing injury and they are no longer able to do the thing they told themselves they were born to do.

The firth one is an imposed identity: like the name suggests, this is when a given identity is imposed upon you by either your family or society. For example, people who are biracial, especially those who are visibly mixed with Black or another race of colour, are often still considered non-White and treated as such.

The sixth one is personal identity: this is the way you regard yourself as an individual, it encompasses your general make up, your gender identity, your pursuits, your habits. Basically, how you have your relationship with yourself. Since this type of identity is very personal, most people struggle here and especially those who have suffered psychological and emotional abuse.

From all these mentioned types of identities, we can deduce that identity in humanity is a static reality and a fluid process. It could be regarded as a state of being and becoming. If we apply this principle to our sense of loss of identity in motherhood, we can say that our self-identity was static before becoming mothers. It is now fluid as we are embracing a new form of our self-identity in motherhood.

In simple terms, your identity is your blueprint, which makes you stand out from the crowd. It encompasses attributes, qualities and values that define how you view yourself, the people around you and the world. We tend to form our identity from the labels we place upon ourselves, the roles we undertake, and the activities we complete. For example, as professional mothers, we can see ourselves as mothers, wives, partners and employees but we need to consider the fact that our identity is shaped from much more than these. It is anchored in our conscious, subconscious and unconscious. Our daily activities, our environment, the people, the things we are exposed to provide us with the experiences which we then internalise. This in turn shapes the way we relate with the world and the people around us. Thus, we essentially identify with whatever resonates with us.

It is worth highlighting that everything we have discussed so far only constitutes the external layer of social phenomena, there is definitely a deeper layer of consciousness, which intensifies the effects of this external layer. This is no other than the collective unconsciousness, [that part of the mind containing memories and impulses of which the individual is not aware] of the society that the psyche is part of. In the same manner personal unconscious [all information that is present within an individual's mind, but not readily available to conscious recall] determines the behaviour of individual, the collective unconscious determine the behaviour of a group of people.

Introduction

Any transition in life can consist of various challenges. Just like all stages in life, some people go through it like a walk in the park whilst others find it more difficult to navigate. Motherhood in and of itself is unfamiliar territory. Like anything new, the preconceived ideas and the reality can be strikingly different. It can alter a woman's self-concept and self-imagine to the extent that she forgets herself. It can cause a sense of loss of control and balance consequently affecting a woman's confidence and personality.

It is commonly understood that after giving birth, the neurological and structural changes in the brain actually cause it to redesign itself. It trims old connections and builds new ones. This can cause a collision between a woman's self- identity and her professional life, which is also another part of her identity.

Admittedly, having a career can be daunting but we have been conditioned or have grown accustomed to it. If you are like me who works the typical 9-5pm shift in an office environment, you can still fit in your social life as well. You can also take advantage of the weekends, whether you have made some plans or not, it is a good thing to have. I can personally say that prior to becoming a mother, I had mastered my routine. Unfortunately, I was oblivious to the fact all of that would change.

As soon as you become a mother, everything changes. It's a tug of war. You now have two jobs which are polar opposites. On one hand, you have your career that you have grown and sustained through hard work, organisation and planning. On the other, you have motherhood where seemingly none of your professional skills are of any use. It doesn't matter how organised you are, being a mother will defeat all your organisation and planning skills. Sadly, this can result in a work / life imbalance, which in turn, can have detrimental effects, to the point where your sense of self is challenged.

This book is dedicated to all women in the world who are juggling motherhood and work, and as a result have suffered a sense of identity loss along the way. We all have our respective journeys; some women may never experience identity loss during this transition. Others may experience it at the onset as a new life has just begun. The rest will experience it later on as they progress on this journey. I am sure if I were to ask each and every single one of you to comment on the subject, you will definitely have an experience to share. Please remember, some of the things that will be discussed in the following pages you may not fully identify with but I hope that we can still have a great conversation.

If you are reading this, I assume that you are either considering starting a family, or you have already started or you are just curious – whatever your reason, you are very welcome.

We have already established earlier that managing both your career and motherhood can be very demanding. The question still remains; is it possible to successfully combine both roles whilst maintaining our self-identity?

Let's talk about it...

Motherhood vs work / career / profession

Generally speaking, there are only four major areas we think about in life. We focus on our career, our education, our family and our friends. The importance attributed to each of the categories depends on the individual. But one thing is certain; modern society tends to prioritise career and education over motherhood. Growing up as a teenager in England, I observed that before the age of 20, my friends and I solely thought of the future in terms of career and education, motherhood did not cross our minds. As we reached 30 or so, we expected to have reached the apex of our careers or at least be well on our way to it, which is an amazing achievement. After 30, was the time, most of us started thinking about settling down or having a family. If things didn't go to plan, the idea was usually relegated to later in life.

As time waits for no one, some of my friends who are now in their 40s reported that since motherhood was not prepared for, it felt as if they had suddenly woken from a coma. They realised that they had invested everything in their careers, they had directed their energies on travel, leisure and pleasure, and although these things were really important, a part of them realised that there were other dimensions to this life. They feel cheated and accuse society of having lied to them, as it sold them the idea that their careers were the thing to focus on in order to live a fulfilled life. This couldn't be further from the truth!

I understand that there are some women who choose not to have children. This is absolutely fine and I respect their choice. I am talking expressly to those who have the desire to have a family but have not made the time for it due to their career and other commitments. I am talking to those women who want to have children but feel discouraged by society. I am also talking to the women who have chosen to have children and pursue their careers.

Our Society does not prepare women for motherhood because it resents the idea! It does not encourage it. It has brainwashed people into thinking that you are better off not being a mother or you can't go further in your career if you were one. It is as if you have been given an ultimatum. You are either a career driven woman or a mother, which is translated as having no ambitions. I am sure you have heard these opinions and comments: they are too many people in the world, so we don't need anymore! Or you don't want to bring a child into this world. Or is it the right thing to bring a child into this terrible world? I appreciate that motherhood is not forced. It is a personal choice and women who choose to become mothers should not be judged or be made to feel small by society. If we are being honest, our career can't be completely fulfilling. Let me explain. We work to get paid, in doing so we are selling our time in return. In other words, we wouldn't be doing our job if there was not a salary involved. It is essentially a financial transaction. It can be deduced that if our jobs didn't pay us, we wouldn't be working at all. This alone contradicts the idea of our career or job being our main source of fulfilment in life. I am not saying that our jobs are not important. I am just trying to paint a picture on our mind so we understand the seriousness of this conversation.

When a woman willingly chooses to become a mother, she is not naïve enough to think that things will be perfect. It is an act of supreme courage in and of itself. She is aware that there will be challenges on the way. She knows that the child will encounter some difficulties; sickness will knock on the door. There could be some financial hardships involved. It could be an emotional rollercoaster. Despite it all, a mother has accepted the responsibilities that come with the role. I couldn't help but think about

Michelangelo's famous sculpture the pieta meaning pity or compassion. This sculpture embodies the sacrifice of a mother, holding her scarified and dead son. It is an image of motherhood, full of sacrifice but at the same time depicts courage and strength. I can only imagine what Michelangelo had in mind while painting it- my only interpretation would be: a mother reliving her entire life from the day her son was born up to this point, when he dies. Most parents hope to be buried by their children and not the other way around. She on the other hand, witnessed her son dying before her. I assume she is feeling guilty and blaming herself for the death of her son. After all, she is the one who brought him into the world. But even in death, the mother chooses to hold her son in love. This is so priceless!

I can relate to this myself. I felt ready to start a family but it was during a very difficult time financially for us. There were so many uncertainties surrounding my daughter's birth. And it was during Covid. People were losing their jobs. Life was restrained on every level. I felt the pressure but I was still determined to have my daughter regardless. Many things were at stake but I turned a blind eye to them. My focus was on her. I knew that there would be certain challenges ahead. I knew that it was going to be demanding. But, I still went ahead. As I understood that there is always a price to pay.

My experience as a mother has taught me three important things that I hadn't realised beforehand.

The first thing is I felt that I finally grew up as a person. It takes great humility and growth to allow someone else to be more important than yourself. I told my family and friends as soon as I gave birth to my daughter, if I had to choose between us, I would choose her every time. I will happily die and let her live. Believe me, I love my life. This thinking only came to me after having experienced motherhood.

The second thing is I learnt to deal with no longer being the centre of attention. As soon as my daughter came into my life, it was as if I didn't exist. Family, friends and even strangers noticed her, they wanted to cuddle her or just smile at her. It doesn't bother me. I believe that it takes great courage to accept the back seat and allow someone else to shine.

Thirdly, I have learnt about other people. My daughter was once a stranger as far as knowing her physically was concerned. Every day, we got to know about each other. I am learning about her, her personality, her habits, her preferences. She is equally learning about me. I have had to make a sort of inventory of my family and friends. I have had to let go of some people, I have re-enforced other friendships and I have created new ones too.

In the same manner that motherhood is a personal choice, being a working mother is also a personal choice. I believe that it is very important to pursue your career as a mother if you desire to. I am definitely one of those who resents the idea that motherhood isn't compatible with a career. As mentioned earlier, I come from a family of 5 children, and I have never seen my own mother take a career break. It was abnormal. I appreciate that it was in a different country and culture, but that's what I was exposed to. It therefore never crossed my mind to consider stopping work because of motherhood either.

Some women choose both their career and family for personal and financial reasons. Others like being away from the home doing something else that is meaningful. Unfortunately, I have come across many women who tend to feel guilty for playing both roles. They tend to think that they are missing out on their children's mile stones or they are not giving their uttermost best. But, I have some good news, according to a 2015 study by Harvard business school professor Kathleen McGinn, their study results showed that the daughters of working mothers were more likely to do better in their careers than those with stay-at-home mothers. They also were 1.21 times to be employed, 1.29 times to have supervisory roles at work, they earned more. Finally, they were happy in adulthood. I sincerely hope you find some comfort in this if you were feeling guilty being a working mother.

Gender bias

Throughout the last 100 years, the world has evolved and is still evolving. Many changes have taken place throughout history. Women are beneficiaries of the positive changes. They have many rights now and a voice which was not the case some time ago. Today, women are employers and employees. They are in business, politics, fashion, media, sports and many other professions. Admittedly, though women have benefited from the changes in the world namely working like their male counterparts, they are still victims of gender biases in the work place and in society. These biases intensify especially when women become mothers. This in turn can affect women's self-identity, which is an integral part of life. Self-identity is very important; it is at the core of our existence. When it is lost, we are essentially lost too. As women with very high ambitions, hopes, aspirations and dreams, we need confidence in ourselves in order to excel in our various endeavours. It is hard enough to be a working woman, when your self-identity can be called into question, let alone a working mother.

As working mothers, we have two roles to play; we are mothers at home and employees at work. This can affect our self–identity even more. The weight of the dual responsibility can be overwhelming. If we are not careful, the confidence we had previously can be shaken and consequently we can lose our identity on the journey.

What is bias?

The Oxford English dictionary defines bias as a strong feeling in favour of or against one group of people, or one side in an argument, often not based on fair judgement.

The same dictionary defines the gender gap as favouritism towards or prejudice against one gender.

Biases are prevalent in our society, they are ingrained in all of us, one way or the other and our upbringing, background and culture, can be some of the contributing factors. These develop into habits, as a result becoming unconscious biases which affect the way we view and treat others. Sadly, these biases can cause us to form prejudices against others, which allows for egregious inequalities to form between different demographics.

I understand that there is a spectrum of gender identities. However, due to the nature of our topic, we will focus on the gender binaries, notably – male and female.

Additionally, there are a number of other types of unconscious bias that disproportionately affect working women's success in the workplace, which include:

> **Performance support bias:** this happens when managers, leaders or colleagues provide more opportunities and resources to a specific gender. They assume that women are more likely

to call in sick or have other family commitments. They tend to train or invest more in male co-workers.

I have experienced this myself when I was returning from maternity leave. For financial reasons, I was planning to resume work very early as I didn't want to succumb to financial pressures. A zoom meeting was scheduled with my boss. I was told that "now you are a mother, you may find it very difficult to adjust. Also, why are you returning to work so early?" I was asked. Basically, my boss didn't even know what the company maternity package included. He assumed that I was still going to be receiving my salary at least for the next six months. I had to explain to him that our organisation only offers Statutory Maternity Pay (SMP). Worst of all, I had to highlight how much it was, he was so shocked. You would think that as a boss and a family man himself, he would know at least the basics! He had no clue. This was appalling to experience. I felt as if I were being judged for deciding to return back to work early.

Performance review bias: this happens when managers, leaders or colleagues review differently both genders' performances. They will view women's performance from a different angle, mostly negative even though they are supposed to review performance based on merit.

I can also relate. Whenever I have had my mid-year review or my end of year appraisal, I can definitely spot the difference between working as a mother and prior to that. My work performance hasn't changed. I have maintained the same work ethic. I meet my targets and deadlines. I really wanted to prove to myself that I could still keep up with my work. However, my boss would always talk to me in a very condescending manner. In the United Kingdom, women are entitled to go on maternity for up to 26 weeks. The conditions must be the same i.e. your initial role and salary should be the same when you return. I appreciate that the money aspect depends on different organisations or companies but there is always SMP as the standard provided by the government. The idea is to be on leave for some time but have your job guaranteed on your return. Conversely, if an employer doesn't accept you back, it is automatically considered unfair dismissal and maternity discrimination. It is worth highlighting that things are improving, men can also go on paternity / parental leave. Also, parental leave can be shared between the couple, should they decide to go down that route.

Now, before maternity leave, I was a team leader. By law in the United Kingdom, your job and title is secured until you return. When I returned I was told that I couldn't manage both roles, being a mother and leading a team. My boss claimed that he didn't want me to sacrifice my family. What? I could see where he was coming from and that he meant well, perhaps he didn't want me to be under pressure. I get that. I then waited until the following year and expressed that I have had enough experience and I had shown that I am capable of maintaining both my family and job. I even added I was working as if no change has happened in my personal life. My boss said, I understand but I will offer you another role instead. Did I mention that my replacement was male? I have nothing against him. However, I know that there were senior women colleagues who could have assumed the role in my absence but they preferred a junior male colleague.

> **Performance reward bias:** this is when managers, leaders or colleagues reward men more frequently and generously than women. This can be seen in promotions and raises. It is no secret that in most places of work, men are preferred over women in terms of promotion and more generous pay raises.

This is regardless of how hard a women works, even when their work outstrips that of male colleagues.

As I've already mentioned, the fact that I couldn't step back into my initial role after my maternity leave had negative effects. It wasn't made obvious in any way however, I know the package I had been given before motherhood, and on my return it was clear to me that my salary, bonuses and raises were viewed in a different light.

This bias is even more noticeable with recruiters. You can see it in the way certain jobs are advertised, you can tell that they are targeted at men! The same can be extended when recruiters can see from your name that you are female. I have encountered this myself when once on the phone, an agent called me. When I picked up the call, he seemed surprised that I was clearly female. Then, he pretended "…Oh, I thought you were French". I am sorry what? What does my nationality, background or gender has to do with the role if I have the expertise?

I must admit, I have also come across certain roles which only consider your expertise. For example, an application form where it specifically states not to put your name or gender. It may also include a competency test where you progress to the next stage is based solely on the test results. I prefer it this way to be honest. As it eliminates certain biases and bases their decision solely on competence, which is fair!

Women are subjected to so many biases in society which makes it very hard sometimes to aim higher in our careers. Try to compete for a given role with a male colleague in your organisation or company and you will see the interrogation you can be subjected to. They ask for your future plan, what they are actually wanting to find out is whether you are considering having a family or if you have, whether they should expect another maternity break! This is revolting!

Looking at the biases mentioned above, there appears to be a glass ceiling when it comes to women excelling and reaching higher in their careers. I ask myself, if these biases do affect women in general in the workplace, how much more so working mothers?

History

We learn from history. It would be unfair to talk about the present without going back in time. We are going to be discussing how women in the past were treated across the globe. We will also learn how women fought against laws and prevailed so that you and I could enjoy certain privileges today.

In almost every society in Africa, Asia, Europe and the Middle East, women did not have any influence over political, cultural or religious matters. They were considered second class citizens, mediocre and good for nothing really. If they were to be put on a scale, they were considered something intermediate between a child and a man. In preceding centuries, land played a major part in families. When a father for instance passed on, the inheritance which could include land would immediately be passed to men. It wouldn't be passed to the descendants if they were women. They could not possess anything; they couldn't own land, property or any form of wealth as they were considered mere objects. We can say that, those material things were put on the same pedestal or had the same value as the women. To make matters worse, in certain cultures they were used as one of the mediums to settle debt. This meant that even if a woman got raped for example, it was not considered a serious matter. They had two ways of handling it. The first one, they could take the rapist's wife and hand her over to the husband of the victim. Secondly, if the wife was taken as a medium of exchanging debt, she couldn't be returned to her husband.

A long time ago, my great grandfather owed a business man some money. The person who he owed kept on asking for his money back, unfortunately at the time, my great grand-father was not able to repay him. As a result, they took my great grand-mother, his wife as a medium to settle the debt. During the time she was with the man, she was raped and got pregnant. When they found out about it, she was returned to my great grand-father and the dispute was resolved. As the pregnancy was kept, a male child was born who later on became my grand-father. It is very sad. The part that really upsets me is the fact that my grand-father was biologically not my grand-father as the pregnancy was dumped on my great-grandfather due to an outstanding debt and his wife had to be used as the transaction to settle it!

In certain Hindu traditions and this is still the case in some part of India, once a husband dies, the wife is considered sinful and incomplete and consequently, she can't remarry. As society con-siders those widows as outcasts, they sometimes see no other way of living than to take their own lives. Some widows, even though it is illegal, choose suttee as the best option. In Hinduism, when someone passes on, the corpse is burnt as part of the funeral cer-emony. The widow throws herself onto her husband pyre –this is known as suttee.

In some parts of the Middle East, women live in seclusion in their own quarters. They are allocated a camp like area where they live and they can't go out unless accompanied by a male relative. In the event that a woman engages in sexual intercourse outside wedlock or is raped, she can be murdered; she is seen as impure and bringing shame to the family.

In Saudi Arabia, women must be dressed in such a way that every single part of their body is covered. They must wear a black gown known as an Abaya that only leaves a slit for their eyes. They are not allowed to drive or ride a bike. If a woman engages in sexual intercourse outside of wedlock or is raped they may be stoned to death as a punishment.

Female genital mutilation occurs across Africa and some parts of Asia. This is where a girl's genitals are cut deliberately between infancy and becoming a teenager, without a medical reason. As you can imagine, it is a very painful procedure and can be very harmful to the health of women and girls. Further, this traumatic experience can have a long term effect on sex intercourse, childbirth and mental health.

Female infanticide is believed to have been common in Europe until recent centuries. It was also dominant in India. Once upon a time, there were more males than females in the population. For cultural reasons in India for example, traditional weddings involve a dowry. The woman's family pays the dowry to the potential husband's family. It can be expensive as items like gold are involved. It is believed that due to the fact that some families are very poor and can't afford it, they opt to kill baby girls instead.

Women were seen as emotional and undisciplined creatures. In other words, they had to be tamed and taught self-control by inflicting violence. Universally, especially in African, wife beating was the norm. There were no repercussions even if it resulted in a fatal injury or even death.

This is believed to have happened in some parts of China, where women were permanently deformed and disabled by having their feet bound as men considered tiny feet erotic. Foot binding consisted of breaking and tightly binding the feet of young girls to change their shape and size. As you can imagine, these practices were excruciating and resulted in lifelong mobility challenges and other disabilities.

Women worldwide throughout the centuries have experienced a saga of violence and oppression meted out by society.

Traditional gender roles have prescribed that the focus of woman's work is motherhood. A woman was a desired object who waited for a man to choose her, thereby giving her status and making her a Mrs. Her primarily role was to be a mother. Throughout history this has always been the case until the 20th century.

The world experienced the first wave of Feminism in the 1920s where women sought their rights through championing motherhood. However, some changes had already begun, through movements likes the suffragettes and their promotion of women's rights, including the right to vote. All of these movements changed the role of women's work and even the definition of what it means to be a woman. As a result, there was a surge in women without children.

After the First World War, there was an assumption that women's temporary roles had been specially linked to wartime. The government encouraged a return to domestic duties.

This movement was affected, in the 1940's by the Second World War, where women were encouraged to work, as so many men were away fighting. However, when the men returned from the war, they reclaimed their place in the world of work. As a result, many women stopped working and reverted to their believed primary role – causing a high surge in family size post the Second World War.

The latter gave rise to the baby boom generation. This is following the silent generation and preceding generation X. This generation is often defined as people born between 1946 and 1964, during the post Second World War era. This generation of women then drove the second wave of feminism in 1960s. They were now demanding their rights through promoting alternatives to motherhood. This was re-enforced by Madison Avenue who launched advertising campaigns for women to return to work.

During this period the world experienced a massive shift in every aspect of civil life. Many issues were challenged such as views on race, sexuality, the meaning of war, gender roles, birth control, abortion rights among others. As ideas have consequences – women, who wanted to exert their right and have children, started having them much later, mostly in their late thirties and forties as a result there was an increase in infertility. Delayed childbearing had become accepted and even fashionable in society. On the other hand, this urban industrialisation created more jobs for women. It was a social and psychological phenomenon.

Our predecessors have fought tirelessly against the things we have mentioned, social injustices and the freedom to be heard and become independent as women. They took matters in their own hands and changed things imposed on them by society. All these movements culminated in the freedoms we enjoy today. Women can now work in leadership positions across the globe despite their gender. Today women occupy prestigious positions in leadership. We occupy every sphere of life. I am grateful to be alive and be one of the beneficiaries today.

As we move forward in our conversation, I want to mention some of the women, past and present, who have inspired me in some way. I appreciate that some of them are complex and controversial just as in any other walk of life.

- Marie Curie who revolutionised the scientific world. She discovered radium and polonium, and she contributed to finding treatments for cancer.

- The Williams Sisters, strong women, dominating the sport of tennis. They are also the world's wealthiest female athletes.

- Mother Theresa a selfless, philanthropic woman. She was a Roman Catholic nun who devoted her life to serving the poor and destitute around the world. Born in Skopje, North Macadonia, she spent many years in India, where she founded the Missionaries of Charity to help to help the poor.

- Rosa Parks, a woman who fought against social injustices. She is known as the mother of the civil rights movement. She stimulated the struggle for racial equality when she refused to give up her bus seat to a white man in Montgomery, Alabama.

- Maya Angelou, a very intelligent poetic voice. She was a poet, dancer, actress, singer, activist, and scholar. She was a world-famous author. She was best known for her unique and pioneering autobiographical writing style.

- Oprah Winfrey, one of the influential and wealthiest women of our time. She is an American television personality, actress, and entrepreneur. Her syndicated daily talk show was among the most popular in the USA.

- Sirimavo Bandaranaike, the first woman prime minister in the world. She was best known for her social work focused on improving the lives of women and girls in rural areas of Sri Lanka. Furthermore, she has won three elections.

- Sakena Yacoobi, an Afghani activist known for her work for promoting access to education for women and children. She is also the founder and executive director of the women-led NGO Afghan Institute of Learning.

- Dame Stephanie Shirley, a German-British information technology pioneer, businesswoman and philanthropist.

- Ngozi Okonjo-Iweala a Nigerian-American economist, fair trade leader, environmental sustainability advocate, human welfare champion. She is also Director-General of the World Trade Organization. She is the first woman and the first African to serve as Director-General.

These women attest by their actions that they wanted to make a mark in the world despite their gender. We also can attest that women are no longer treated like subordinates or maids who belong only in the kitchen. Women won't tolerate any ill treatment by society anymore because they know better. We are leading on every level. We are educated. We matter. We are role models. We are influential.

I am aware that there are still some aspects that need to be addressed and amended as you are well aware, women are still fighting injustices such as sexism, the gender pay gap and biases as discussed earlier.

The 2016 film Hidden Figures exemplified this. It is based on a true story of the events of US and Russian race to put the first man in orbit. A team of female African American mathematicians served a role in NASA during the conception of this programme. These women though talented and incredibly smart had to deal with racial and gender discrimination at work. The film graphically portrays the biases women encounter in the work place.

Also, the story of Dame Stephanie Shirley, after creating her software programme business in 1962, she had to sign her business letters with the pseudonym Steve as when she signed with her real name, Stephanie, people seldom responded.

We have seen that women can occupy prestigious positions in society today. The pertinent question remains: can becoming a mother affect women from thriving in the work place? Are we going to let status –quo and motherhood prejudice take its toll? Sadly, it is common to see that some companies and organisations do not have any maternity leave arrangements or anything pertaining to maternity in place. It is not impossible to see some jobs that will not encourage women to progress when they are of a certain age for fear of the same. This is also evident in some working women who are feeling the pressure to avoid motherhood altogether for fear of their roles or packages being affected. After investing so much in their jobs or companies, it is very understandable. Who builds something and expects someone else to reap the benefits? One sows to reap, not to hand it over for free. I am not here to judge. We as women ultimately have the choice to either conceive to raise a child or choose to adopt one whilst working or not at all. I personally think that Western culture doesn't really facilitate this, as a result many women have relegated the idea to the realm of fantasy.

Childbirth

Since we are talking about mothers, I feel it is also fitting to touch a little on childbirth itself. It is a good idea to remind ourselves about it.

Now then, childbirth is the process of giving birth to a baby. As you know, this involves the act of giving. When I give you something, there's a loss on my part but a gain on your part. Therefore, it is important to understand when you have given birth, you have donated a part of yourself which you will never regain.

On the same note, the term motherhood refers to the condition of being a mother, which is associated with giving birth, and from this term we have another familiar phrase mothering. This evokes images of nurturing and caring for a child. Thus, to be a mother, doesn't necessarily involve giving birth. You can be a stepmother. You can become a mother through adoption. You can be a foster mother.

As soon as I gave birth to my daughter, the midwife asked if I wanted some skin-to-skin time with my baby before they cleaned her up. Of course, I couldn't wait to hold my daughter. As they laid her tiny body on me, I felt so accomplished at that moment; I was so joyful to meet this unknown creature who has been the object of my imagination for nine months. Nine months in which I could only imagine what she would look like, and now I was actually seeing her face to face. I was elated that we had finally met. It made me feel like a superstar. If you had told me that the world was going to end then, I won't have been bothered. I felt so complete!

Then, the fun began. I was left alone with this new creature, my mood veered from "I did it" to the shock of my life. Disbelief at the changes in my body, from my tummy looking like I was still pregnant, my swollen feet to my sore breasts filled with milk that wouldn't come out. Most importantly the question…

What do I do now?

I was very confused. I have never travelled down this road before. Many thoughts raced through my mind. Many unanswered questions.

Up until this time, my focus was just on my daughter. As time passed by, I started to get a feel for things. I was learning as I went along. I was getting used to the process and gaining confidence in my new role day by day. I always had my check list: milk every two hours or feed on demand, nappy change, bath time, hopefully she sleeps and that's when I tried to sleep as well. Washing this and that, ironing clothes, appointments here and there to make sure I was doing what was expected of me. There was always something I had to do. It was at this point that I realised the true meaning of, "for better for worse". I remember taking my vows at the altar when I got married but I hadn't quite understood. Real understanding only came with motherhood. I had to become the nurse when she was unwell. I was everything to her. I realised that all I became was a mother, nothing more and nothing less, and especially a milk factory as I laughingly called myself.

Childbirth

I was on maternity leave and a part of me was relieved that at least for a few months I wouldn't have to worry about meetings, emails, or work in general – even a little glad that I wasn't going to be seeing certain faces. Of course, no more rushing early in the morning to catch the busy trains! However, sleepless nights became the norm. Constant headaches and tiredness were my bread and butter. This is when I asked myself "is this all I am now?" I would say my self-identity was taking a profound knock.

Whether you are a new mother or plan on becoming one, I salute you. Managing both work and a child is not an easy task. It can be very challenging. I want to assure you that you are definitely not abnormal if you are feeling like you have lost yourself. Many other women have been there and others will come after us. As long as life continues on earth, there will be mothers. They will also experience loss of identity.

The things we will be discussing are designed as a guide to help you use certain strategies that have helped me and other women who have already walked this path. We did it and these things successfully helped us overcome certain insecurities and dogmas associated with this topic of identity loss.

Admittedly, we can all agree that unless you are a supernatural being, your body will not look the same at least not after just giving birth. The female body is subjected to many changes which can be due to genetic predisposition, age, diet, hormones, birth control measures to name but a few. Though, subconsciously we know that our bodies are constantly undergoing changes, we seem to be terrified to face the reality. Let me explain, after giving birth, your body may not return to its original size. In some cases, our genetic predisposition can cause changes to our bodies such as weight gain, stretch marks, and a bigger shoe size are changes you may experience. This is what the people around us see, the exterior. Their comments in turn can add fuel to our already existing insecurities. In other cases, some women have come to terms with the exterior insecurities by accepting their new selves. But, they could be struggling with the internal insecurities. This is the hardest thing to overcome, in my opinion, since it is embedded in us and no one else can see them. I have come across some women who appeared very confident on first meeting, but after spending some time with them, I saw the real woman. When the mask was removed I could see the vulnerable person loaded with unresolved past experiences.

That being said, other factors can play a huge part, they can be psychological, physiological, or financial, to list but three. Depending on the person, this shock to the system can be severe and have serious consequences. It is not uncommon for women to suffer from postnatal depression or postnatal anxiety. If this resonates with you, please know that you are not being judged but rather saluted for your hard work. The purpose of this book is to discuss certain factors which can contribute to a working mother's identity loss and what can be done to overcome it.

It is believed that you can't take anyone where you have not been. I have collected data from other women who kindly shared their experiences and also provided us with some tips that we can all draw from. You are in for a treat. No one knows it all-there is always room to learn or be reminded to do certain things. I want you to know that though it may feel like you are walking alone or going through this time alone, other people have been where you are now. There is nothing new under the sun. My aim at the end of this book is for you to be equipped to face this issue so you can awaken the lioness within. I really believe that what will be shared in the following pages will be a reminder which will help you change your life for the better and live as a happy woman within and without.

Change

Nature teaches us that there is always change happening around us. The weather changes constantly. The seasons change. In temperate climates, we expect to see spring, summer, autumn, and winter. They are all different and happen at different times. When they don't happen as expected, we tend to complain.

Our everyday lives are changing. Years ago, the phones we used were trendy, now they are obsolete and of no value. We didn't always have social media. It was very hard and expensive to make international calls. People used to communicate with letters. It used to take months to sail from one country to another. Today, we fly. A 30-day voyage then will take a matter of hours now. We didn't have refrigerators, today it is the most used gadget in our kitchens. We went from driving vehicles to now having driverless ones. The change is ever constant. Innovation and creativity are the new currency. Everything is evolving.

    Change is uncomfortable
    Change is painful
    Change is work
    Change is a chore
    Change is unattractive
    Change is overwhelming
    Change is difficult
    Change is sacrificial
    Change is inevitable.

Human beings naturally resist change. It doesn't matter whether it is a good change or a bad change, our first reaction is to say no.

I usually take delight in rearranging my house. I will arrange the furniture in my living room, or just add some nice decorations. It changes the mood in the house. It feels very nice and I enjoy doing it. I only enjoy doing it because I am in control of the changes. The change is not significant. If I am not happy with the new arrangement, I can always change it back. It doesn't feel like I have lost anything. Now, if we were talking about a massive change, that's an entirely different ball game. For instance, if I were to relocate to a new country, I would be very nervous. I might even talk myself out of the idea by considering several things. I have a child now, is it wise to go somewhere new where I don't know anyone? What if there is an emergency? What if I don't like it? What happens if I need help with childcare? Can you see how my brain starts playing? It will focus on every possible negative outcome.

But, what if I could train my brain to think the exact opposite? Wouldn't that be great?

Let's practice. I am relocating to a completely new city. Well, how exciting? I wonder what great opportunities await me there. It is true that I don't know anyone but I will definitely make new friends. When it comes to child care, surely there are great childminders or nurseries there as well. Now, can you see how the same situation has been completely altered when another perspective has been applied?

Now, let's step this up. How comfortable are you when you are faced with a very important decision to make? Changing job for example, when you have been around your current one for a very long time? Are you one of those people who would just put up with their jobs even though everything around them suggests that it is time to move on? Most of the time, People are too comfortable to leave the familiar and fear thinking about new ventures. The idea of change can be terrifying. They come up with excuses and reasons which create a mental block whenever the topic comes up. They say things like, everywhere is the same you know. Or, at least I know how everything works in my current job. They use terms like, "the devil you know is better than the angel you don't know". The translation is simply they are scared to leave their comfort zone.

With motherhood, I would suggest we shift our mind-set completely. Yes, it is a new adventure. It may not be a comfort zone. It may be rocky at times. You may feel like you are not good at it. You may even feel like you are acting a role, but take heart. It is challenging because it's not a familiar situation. Regardless, let's also consider the innumerable benefits associated with motherhood. Let's take stock and count the blessings associated with it. It just takes the right perspective to start approaching the entire experience positively. Perhaps it is due to the fact that we are not fully in control of the change and we feel like we have lost ourselves. Or maybe we should just accept the fact that this change is permanent and though we may not fully be in control, we can still control the outcomes. Let's make the best out of the situation.

Sometimes we tend to ignore the seemingly inconsequential things associated with motherhood, things like a cuddle from your child or that grin on their face when you walk across the room. Girl, these just melt my heart. I will tell you a funny story. I booked to go on a course for three consecutive days some time ago. Children weren't allowed. Childcare was arranged accordingly. This was the first time I had ever left my daughter with someone else. It felt very strange not to have her around. I was constantly checking up on her and my friend was very gracious. She kept me posted about everything she was up to, when she ate or when she had a nap. At the end of the first day, I went to pick her up. As soon as I walked in the room, she just ignored me. I kept on calling her but she didn't really care. Oh, I was heartbroken. That wasn't the scenario I'd rehearsed in my head. I assumed since she hadn't seen me all day, she would jump up and run towards me. I just sat down and said to my friend, I don't think my daughter cares. After a few minutes, she came to me and started kissing and hugging me. I was in paradise. You see, it was an entirely new experience for my daughter and for me. She needed time to process the situation before she could react. I, on the other hand, lacked the patience or understanding to allow her to do this. This is what we do to ourselves. We want things to go our way whereas we need to allow the process to take its course. We need to be patient and everything will eventually fall into place.

Exposure

I appreciate the word exposure has some negative connotations. However, here I am using it to talk about experiences. One has to be exposed to certain realities to unlock the mind. Exposure makes you curious. Once you are exposed to something new you aren't the same. This reminds me of my daughter. She is fascinated by anything new she comes across. She will see a pebble on the sea-shore, she will pick it up and examine it as if she has seen something precious, like gold. I am observing but she won't let me distract her. She is too busy contemplating this marvellous discovery. She will not stop there; she will then try to taste it. She uses her five senses to grasp the entire concept 'pebble'. She does this at home as well, I will be feeding her some delicious meal I have prepared with all your heart, then, she will ignore this feast but pay attention to a tiny grain of rice on the floor. She is more interested in that. Our home or the outside world exposes her mind to thousands of things which trigger her curiosity.

I remember as a little girl on the streets of Congo, I was exposed to international television channels, music and fashion. I grew up watching other cultures from afar but at the same time attempting to conform to my own culture. Every time I saw Western culture on television, it portrayed love, the good life, the latest gadgets, the best cars and a great body imagine. The image I had of the West was just incredible. I never thought that there were homeless people. I didn't know there were beggars too. I didn't know there was gang violence. I didn't know that there were teenage pregnancies. So, when I moved to the United Kingdom I was exposed to the real reality. I started noticing discrepancies with the images I had forged in my mind while growing up.

In moving to the United Kingdom and living in London, a cosmopolitan city, I was exposed to a new language, cuisine, and culture. Also, whilst at university, I was exposed to other cultures; I studied with people from every race, background and religion. I was exposed to a larger and completely different demographic and culture. Where I grew up in Africa, the majority of the people were natives. The handful of foreigners I knew were either tourists or business people. We had nothing in common – the only interaction we had was a greeting whenever we stepped in their shops. The Major religion practiced in Congo is Christianity and there are strong Muslim communities. However, my exposure to any other religion, is what we studied in history at school.

During my time as a waitress a few years back, I was only trained to set tables, serve food and beverages to clients. This was a no brainer, as I did this at home. Then, I was trained to do Silver-Service also known as French Service. This an entirely new method of food service. As you can imagine, the calibre of guest you cater for has very high expectations. First of all, you smile and welcome the guests, you offer to take their coats or bags to the cloak room. You take them to their allocated seats. You pull out the chair for them, they sit down. You then place napkins on their laps. You then ask what drink they would like to have. The principal guest is served first. Later, the waiting staff transfers food from a serving dish to the guests' plates, always from the left. You do this by using service forks and spoons. There is an order to follow as to what is placed on their plate. This again exposed me to another dimension in catering.

I use all the above examples to emphasise the fact that when our brain is exposed to something new, it changes. You can't un-see something you have seen. A seed has been planted, and you can't erase the experience from your memory.

I believe that the way our society is designed, prevents women from having children. There are extraordinary expectation placed on these women, they have to compete with their male counterparts (who are not directly affected if they choose to be parents). These women are under pressure, they expect to excel in their careers but at the same time, society expects them to look good. For example, you wouldn't see a male leader being criticised for the way he dresses while delivering a speech for example. If you are a woman leader, everything about you and everything you do, is monitored. You have to look a certain way, dress a certain way, you have to wear makeup – basically look feminine. It becomes very difficult for certain women to even think about motherhood. They have so much to lose career wise that they would rather remain childless. As a result, we are not exposed to the idea of being able to succeed in both motherhood and our careers. I can say that role models are scarce.

Women business executives, doctors, lawyers, academics, and parliamentarians are rarely mothers.

Let's name a few high-profile recent examples:

- Angela Markel, former Chancellor of Germany

- Theresa May, former England's Prime Minister

- Nicola Sturgeon, First Minister of Scotland

- Condolezza Rice, former United States Secretary of States

- Oprah Winfrey, talk show host, producer, writer and actor.

I am sure you can name others…

There are always exceptions. It would be unfair not to mention those women of influence who have been able also to embrace motherhood. I couldn't help but talk about the royal family.

- Queen Elizabeth II has four children. She has been on the throne for 70 years this year. This trend has been followed by the family.

- Kate Middleton has three children and Meghan Markle has two children.

- Ngozi Okonjo-Iweala, we saw her earlier, the director-General of the World Trade Organization has four children

- Baroness Karren Brady, business executive tycoon and television personality has two children

- In 25 January 1990 Bakhtawar Bhutto Zardari, Pakistan prime minister was the first woman in the world to give birth while still in the office.

- In 21 June 2018, Jacinda Ardern New Zealand's Prime Minister gave birth while still in the office. This made her only the second elected leader in modern history to give birth while in office.

I don't know about you but I am impressed by these last two women. They are true testament that being a mother shouldn't prevent you from rising to the top in your field of endeavour. Being in politics is stressful. People look to you. As a leader, you are responsible for so many lives and your decisions are vital, they can make or break a nation. These women did their jobs and also chose motherhood.

I just hope that we will be exposed to more role models like Queen Elisabeth, Kate Middleton, Meghan Markel, Bakhtawar Ngozi Okonjo-Iweala, Bhutto Zardari, and Jacinda Ardern so that we can have the courage to enjoy motherhood and pursue our careers.

I believe that when an idea becomes common, it creates more awareness and can give a sense of hope to those aspiring to become something or do something. As a working mother I want to see examples of other women who have managed to combine both roles and succeeded in their lives. I want to be encouraged to pursue my aspirations and dreams by having a role model to aspire to. Perhaps you and I can be featured next on the list of those who have been able to successfully manage work and motherhood, and in turn show other women the way!

Loss of Identity in Motherhood

I particularly chose this topic for us to discuss because it hits home. I experienced identity loss when I became a mother. Also, many people in my circle have suffered identity loss. This, encouraged me to initiate a conversation, like we are having right now.

I attended one of Evolving butterflies' talk on love. It is a women's event run by a very good friend of mine whose mission is to impact women by providing the space to be free to talk about sensitive topics. Many things were said. At the end of the session, there was a Q&A. One of the questions posed to the speaker was, "what do you do when you feel like you have lost your identity as a woman after having a child?".

It may not seem like a big deal, however something within me reacted. You know, at times something needs to happen to awaken you. To cause you to reflect on something dear to you or to simply realise that you have perhaps been operating on autopilot and didn't even have a clue that you had an issue or a concern. As mentioned earlier, I knew that my life was taking a different turn when on maternity leave. But, after attending this talk on love, it was as if I were reminded that I had relegated that feeling. It wasn't being addressed.

I was driving home and the question kept reverberating in my head. I realised something, my identity was at risk or could be at risk if I didn't take action or at least acknowledge it. This then caught my attention and I became very curious to finding out from other fellow working mothers at different stages of their lives and get more insight.

Before I proceed, it is very important to remind ourselves that there is always a cause and an effect. Nothing in our lives happens randomly. There is always an underlying or unresolved issue from our past. Loss of self – loss of identity can be linked to issues from the past, from childhood, childhood bullying, parental neglect, from abuse or trauma. This often shapes how we view ourselves and how we interact with others. These feelings can be re-triggered by major life events or a particular change in your circumstances such as becoming a mother.

Some people are completely oblivious to it but they could have a longing for social acceptance and reassurance from others. You want to be heard, you want to be noticed, you want to be loved, you want to feel like you are wanted, you want to be cared about. That issue may not even be your fault but as we know life just happens. As human beings in general, we tend to suppress certain feelings to avoid perhaps shame, disappointment, being judged or not being accepted. You could have gone through some form of abuse whether sexual or verbal as a young person or a child and you just grew up choosing to erase that part of your life. These dormant memories are unpleasant and bring up some form of regret or resentment. Consequently; you could have developed insecurities about yourself. You may think that you are not good enough. You could be judging everything you do as a mother in a negative light.

A very close friend of mine was raped as a teenager. Though many years have passed by she has never been stable in her relationships.

Every man is viewed as a potential perpetrator. She constantly feels like she is not worthy of love. She feels so damaged. When she became a mother, it was as if water was stirred and all the hidden issues re-surfaced. She was judging herself as a mother. Nothing she did was good enough. Even when she was complimented, she thought the compliment was not sincere. This is what could happen when past unresolved issues have not been dealt with.

Now, as a new mother, you have new challenges but since you never dealt with your past issues; like my friend, the new challenges and the old memories mingle. This creates a recipe for disaster. You may feel lethargic about life and feel like you are exploding with issues. Suddenly you go from being a very confident woman to being a very fearful one. You just can't cope. You go from someone who is very driven and focused to someone with shaky motivation who questions everything. Consequently, you lose confidence and start to judge everything you do. As a mother, you don't feel worthy to be one. As the unresolved issues re-emerge, your brain transfers the same feeling to the new stress from motherhood. Before you felt that you were not good enough as an individual, now as a mother you have convinced yourself of the same thing. You must be a bad mother too. This is why it is very important you deal with past experiences and trauma to create room for the new life you have embarked on.

You can't fill an already full bottle of water. The water will go to waste. The only sensible thing to do is to empty the bottle first, then re-fill it with fresh water. Please, if you have any unresolved issues from your past, deal with them. Seek help to make room for the new experience in your life.

Research

I designed a survey targeting new working mothers to find out whether they had experienced any sense of identity loss at some point in their lives.

Objectives

- To investigate women's experiences of identity change or loss during their transition from womanhood to motherhood.

- To determine whether the dual responsibility as a mother and working professional impact self-identity

- To determine and compare the coping strategies adopted by working mothers to combat loss of self-identity.

Design
I designed a survey which contained the following questions:

1. Upon becoming a mother, did you at any point feel like your identity was lost?
2. If yes, when did you realise it?
3. How was your life impacted?
4. Did you speak to anyone about it?
5. How did you get back on track?

The survey was sent to all of my friends and acquaintances who identify as working professionals.

Demographic characteristics of the participants
Thirty women ranging from twenty eight to forty years old, having children 0-4 years old

With this in mind, let's dive into our topic.

I'll share both my answers and those offered by participants.

1. Upon becoming a mother, did you at any point feel like your identity was lost?

...Feeling like being in a trance
I personally did not call it identity loss at first as I was still in a trance. I have been working full time since I graduated from university. I got married but I was very independent. It didn't feel like I was missing anything. I was still able to enjoy my life and do what made me happy. I was always out and about. Though I was married, it didn't feel like anything had changed in my social life. I still made it to every office outing. I still attended friends' birthday dinners and celebrations. I still travelled abroad- well that was pre-covid! What I am trying to say is, I still felt like I was me. I didn't feel at any point that I had lost myself. This also resonated with some of the women I spoke to. They felt as if it was an out of body experience and at the same time, it was gradual until they finally realised something was happening to them.

...Feeling of emptiness
One of the women said that she felt empty. It was like a void was created during her maternity leave. She did not know what to do about it. I can definitely identify with this. Now, I went on maternity

leave at thirty-eight weeks – two weeks before my due date. As soon as I left work, I felt empty. I was planning and preparing for my daughter's arrival but I still wanted to be busy. I was told that it was "nesting". It is a motherly instinct which prepares you for the baby. I felt I was travelling on empty streets with so many uncertainties.

…Losing the wheels on the car
One of the women described the experience like losing the wheels on her car. It was chaotic. I can also identify with this. Fast forward, I had a routine even while pregnant. When my daughter got here, I felt as if I had lost the wheels on the car as well. Everything shifted drastically. It was as if I didn't know who I was anymore. Please don't get me wrong, I am not saying that I wasn't excited – I was indeed elated but the experience made me feel I had lost control.

…No longer in the picture and felt alone
One of the women felt like she was no longer in the picture. It was very painful as she felt erased. She couldn't remember anyone whether relatives or friends wanting to find out how she was doing. Every visit, phone call or text she received was solely about her daughter. Even when she was exhausted! This was exactly how I felt also. I love my daughter but it felt like I was no longer in the picture. I know it does sound selfish but I just wanted to feel like I was still Noelle. You know?

Added to that while still on maternity leave, my daughter was at the centre of everything, I didn't know who to speak to or complain to or just vent! I wanted to be checked up on too. I wanted to share the attention. Whenever I attempted expressing it, I was told jokingly, "it is all about your daughter", "who cares about you?" … I know it wasn't serious and my family and friends didn't mean harm but I was hurt, just a bit. In my head a different tune was playing. As a result I felt alone at times. It sound very strange because I was around people but yet still felt lonely.

…Loss of independence
One of the women mentioned she felt she'd completely lost her independence. She couldn't do anything without her daughter. She felt she was on surveillance 24/7. To do a simple chore was impossible but at the same time, you were still required to do everything to care for yourself and the baby.

…Felt like a docile cow ready for milking
One of the women described another aspect of losing her body with breastfeeding. Her baby was solely on breast milk and she felt exhausted. I can completely relate to this. My daughter was on both breast milk and formula but I knew she preferred the former. Thus I was breastfeeding on demand which really affected my energy levels. I felt like a docile cow ready for milking whenever my daughter cried. I lost autonomy over my body – as if it didn't belong to me anymore.

…Sleep deprivation
One of the women said that she used to love her sleep but she could control when she wanted to sleep. Then, when her baby came along, she couldn't get a good night's sleep. This caused insomnia which lasted for a very long time. I didn't suffer from insomnia but my sleep pattern was so out of synch. Prior to becoming a mum, I slept when I felt like it. I could stay up late by choice. I did not need permission from anyone to do anything. You get what I mean? I appreciated that this drama only lasted a few months but it was very hard during those early days.

…Loss of routine
The majority of the mothers I spoke to said that they had lost their normal routine. Especially since having a job gave them a

sense of routine. This disturbance affected every aspect of their lives as you can imagine. A routine gives us a sense of direction. When this is lost, we can feel lost too. I can identify with this as well. I completely lost my everyday routine. I had to re-learn certain things and unlearn others.

...Loss of social life
A great number of the women stated that the social aspect of their lives was affected. They couldn't indulge in activities they were able to before. For example, they couldn't go out for a drink after work with colleagues or just be spontaneous about taking a trip. This lack of social interaction made them feel like they were just mothers but nothing else. I can also relate to this. When I became a mother, my social life was almost extinct. Every invitation from friends and colleagues were respectfully declined. Plus, I hardly had any energy in me to be honest.

We can all agree that social life plays a huge part in our lives and of course to in our self-identity as well. I couldn't help but think about the pandemic. We saw how the rate of suicides and depression surged in society. As human beings, we are designed to live in communities so when we gather as a group of friends or work colleagues, it releases dopamine. Also emotional beings, we find comfort in talking to one another – whether we are complaining, gossiping or just being silly, we release stress in the process.

...A shadow in society
A woman said that she felt like a shadow in society. She felt invisible and out of reach. All she had become was just someone's mum. She attempted to give clues to her friends and family, she was crying for help but nobody could see her. She just wanted to be considered and not to have to compete for attention with the baby.

...Craved for old self

A woman said that although she was happy when she became a mother- she is still craving for her old self at times. She added she wished she could turn back the clock to be herself again one more time. I must admit that there were times I felt like that as well. It can be very difficult to realise and accept that once you have lost your old self in motherhood, there is literally no way of return. It is like purchasing a one way train ticket or driving on a one way street.

...Forgotten by society

Some women highlighted that people stopped referring to them as individuals. This affected their persona. It gave them the impression of being outcast and not belonging in society. The fact that everyone in their circle was aware that they had become mothers emphasised the sense of identity loss. Everything and anything appeared to revolve only around it- any question asked was always related to the baby. I can also identify with this. I still wanted to be addressed as myself. I didn't like any remarks which pointed out I was no longer myself.

...Baby glued on you

My daughter was very clingy when she was younger. She always wanted to be held. When she was asleep, she wanted to feel my touch, otherwise she would wake up. I was constantly with her and it was draining. It was as if she was glued on me. Other women also reported the same.

2. If yes, when did you realise it?

...On maternity leave

Some women pointed out that the realisation occurred during maternity leave. The change in their routine or its lack made it feel as though they were lost. I can identify as well. I felt lost during my maternity leave. It was a new adventure which I was not prepared for.

...Baby's arrival
Some women said that when their babies actually were born. Everything was upside down. Everything in their lives was shaken. They didn't know how to cope with the new arrival. There were some mixed emotions. Their babies brought so much joy in their families. At the same time, they felt like looking after their babies was all they had become.

...Returning to work
Some women reported they felt inadequate when they returned to work after maternity leave. They felt like aliens. They found it very challenging to resume work and concentrate on their jobs. I can identify with this myself. I was nervous to resume work after maternity leave. I didn't know what to expect when I returned. I remember having a meeting with my boss after expressing my desire to resume work. We were then trying to strategize and devise a plan. We both agreed that I could come back on a temporary basis and see how it went. Once I felt more comfortable, we would review the plan again.

...Not knowing how to be an employee again
A woman reported she had lost the ability to be an employee. She had forgotten her skills. This sounds very familiar. To be frank with you, I was not sure either how I was going to be an employee again. It sounds strange but it is true. I have had time off work before. The only difference with this one was that I was returning as a mother.

...Dual role
Some women reported that they were unsure how things were going to work out being a mother and working professional. I personally

dreaded the idea of entertaining both roles. My head was ready to resume work but my heart was not. The fight within was surreal.

…Underperforming
Some women reported that their performance at work was affected. They tended to judge everything they were doing. Before becoming a mother, they had been able to complete a given task quite easily. After, it felt as if there was a mental block. I personally became slower at the beginning; I just took longer to get back on track. I am a Senior Analyst and I deal with sensitive information which requires great attention to detail. I wasn't quite sure whether I was going to be able to adapt to the new person I had become.

…Couldn't cope with expected demands
Some of the women reported that the pressure was just too much. They were able to handle the pressure before except now, things appeared much more difficult. Before becoming a mother, working under pressure was second nature. They expected to tackle motherhood the same way but failed miserably.

…Shock of a life time
Some women reported, it was as if they were submerged into icy water which woke them up from sleep. They felt so unprepared for the process.

…Made redundant
Some women unfortunately were made redundant after becoming mothers. They believe that their employers considered them as liabilities.

…No flexible work
Some women felt they needed more flexibility with work as mothers. They expressed the idea to their employers but it

wasn't forthcoming. As a result, some decided to change careers altogether.

3. How was your life impacted?

...Relationships were affected
Some women reported their relationship in general was affected. They didn't have time for anything else nor anyone else. I found it extremely difficult during the early stages. I think it gets better with time. As for my relationship with my family, I am in a good place. My life was and still is impacted socially. I am a very bubbly and lively person. I was always around my friends. Sadly, the stage I am at, at the moment doesn't permit me to do the things I used to do with ease. Let me give an example. A group of friends will plan to meet but they wouldn't tell me about it. I will only find about it after it has happened. If I ask my friends, they say, "Well, we didn't think you could make it." As trivial as this example may seem, the fact remains that I am now viewed differently by some of my friends.

...Work was affected
Many women I spoke to said that their jobs were impacted after they became mothers. They had to incorporate their children into their new routine. I can identify with this totally. When I am working now, I can't start or finish when I like. I have to drop or pick up my daughter from nursery. As soon as work finishes, I have to attend to my family's need. Sometimes, I have to make up my hours at work if I had to run off earlier than usual the day before. This will mean, either missing lunch or staying up very late.

...Social life affected
We have already seen how important social life is. Most of the mothers agreed with me that before the baby's arrival we were

able to attend every social activity after work. To attempt this exercise now requires so much planning. For example, the activity has to take place on a day that my husband is either off or finishing work earlier. If it is not a good day for him, I have to ask around friends and relatives to see who might be available to babysit. If this doesn't work, a childminder will have to be contacted. The bottom line is, it is very time consuming trying to organise childcare outside of working hours. Besides, people have their own lives to deal with as well. Clearly, I avoid all this hassle and don't attend the activity.

Some mothers also highlighted that as much as they would like to respond to every invitation, they can't as most of the activities or events aren't child friendly. It means needing to confirm childcare arrangements before accepting the actual invitation. We all agreed that our lives as mothers are pretty much led by our children.

…Lost friends

We all agreed that our lives changed shape. We were not as reliable when it came to certain things. Thus, we all lost some friends mostly because they didn't identify with the new person we had become. Anything we said, felt like we were not putting in much effort. For example, unlike before, we couldn't be on the phone for a long time. We promise to return the call but forget to do so. Or we get a call but can't hear as our children have put the phone on mute or cancelled the call as they were watching YouTube. All these sound like excuses but in reality they are not.

…Depression

Some women I spoke with said that they became depressed. Others became even clinically depressed. They had postnatal depression and postnatal anxiety.

These are very sensitive topics and I have had first-hand experience on how these can affect someone from very close people in my circle. I will expand on this a bit later.

…Relationship with spouses / partners affected
Some women reported that their relationship with spouses/ partners was affected. Whenever they attempted explaining the experience of feeling a sense of loss to their partners or spouses, it felt like they didn't understand.

…Divided attention
Some women mentioned that they had forgotten how to be a wife or a spouse to their husbands or partner. They felt that the baby was draining all their energy and attention and they had none left over for their relationship. They lost the desire for intimacy. Thus, in some cases, partners felt neglected which caused more misunderstanding in their homes.

…Easily irritable
Some women reported that the lack of sleep that comes with the job of being a mother affected their mood. They became easily irritated. Their entire system was affected; it took from a few months up to a year for some of the women to regain normal sleep. We know the importance of sleep, when we are deprived of it, things don't go well. Thus, some woman complained of having constant headaches and overall body pain.

…Out of sync
Most of us agreed that we lacked time and balance. We felt out of synch most of the time. We just didn't know how to manage everything. Finding balance is essential to function. At the end of the day, you are only one individual with so many things needing

your attention. It is therefore vital to reach that place in your life where you are completely balanced.

4. Did you speak to anyone about it?

…Spoke to partners / spouses
Many women said they reached out to their spouses and partners. They also reported that the experience was in itself therapeutic. It gave them the confidence to rely on the support system around them.

I spoke to my husband on many occasions, interestingly enough, I found that he had his own insecurities too, around the entire fatherhood process. It was very encouraging to see that I was not the only one struggling. As difficult as it is to realise but some men have their own share of loss of identity during fatherhood. It makes sense completely when I think about it. Whether you are a new father or mother, transitioning into parenthood can be very challenging. There is so much expectation, this can create enormous pressure. The conversations with my husband really provided me with a completely fresh perspective. It made me feel better about myself. It did bond us as we realised that we needed each other's support to make it through.

My husband and I would share our worries, concerns and fears related to our parenting and devise a plan. This always worked for us. We had to set certain goals just to measure our progress. This was an eye opener for me and it made things simpler. It gave me more reasons to open up more about any other concerns that arose. I have come to realise the more my daughter is growing, the different and even the more complex certain issues are becoming. Having a non-judgemental support system, allows me to be free and just vent if need be.

...Spoke to friends and family
Many women advised speaking to family and friends. They found it very helpful when an older mother advised them on something related to motherhood. They agreed that most of the issues related to motherhood were common to others.

Some mothers also claimed that the entire motherhood experience and especially talking to their biological mothers more, have brought them closer. Not all of them had a great relationship with their mothers growing up. The conversations were scarce but now there is always something to discuss regarding their children. So, becoming mothers had helped them understand certain things they hadn't understood from their past. Their children had offered the healing that was needed. They can now depend on their mothers and as a result they feel more confident to mother their own children.

I also reached out to my family and friends when I struggled with motherhood. Since most of them are mothers, it was very helpful. I found that I didn't need to re-invent the wheel. Any issue I had was not new – someone amongst them had surely been there before. It was very important for me to rely on their experiences. It facilitated things for me. There were times when I will panic about something with my daughter – I recall one event, my daughter was grunting, to me it was an unfamiliar sound. I could feel that she was in pain. I went on google – like any millennial mother would do, to try to find out how I could be of assistance to my little girl. I couldn't find anything concrete. My husband was sleeping peacefully, as if nothing was happening. Oh boy, did I lose it that night! I started shouting at my husband: "how can you be so selfish and sleep when I have to deal with everything myself? Can't you see she is not fine and you don't care? I went on and on. With hindsight, it was unnecessary; I was the one panicking and was selfish. How will my husband not sleeping fix the situation?

Anyway, I called 111, that's our emergency medical help-line service, in case you are reading this outside the United Kingdom. They said that it was not that serious and it will go on its own. I still wasn't convinced. I called all the mothers in my circle to complain about my husband insensitivity and 111 not being helpful. The first one I called started laughing. This made me even madder. She continued, 111 was right. New born grunting is common and is usually related to digestion as they are getting used to consuming milk either formula or breastmilk. Well, I am pretty sure the mother I spoke to had a similar experience, that's why she could confidently detect the issue and offer the help I needed at the time. Things like this really encouraged me to open up to experienced mothers. I am in my thirties but a mother who started having children earlier even if they are much younger than me, would be more exposed to motherhood and know things I wouldn't know.

At my work place, there are a few mothers who have been where I am. It was very helpful to hear their experiences especially work related. So anytime I needed some advice about motherhood, they were my point of call. I relied immensely on their experiences and expertise and just applied the things they had recommended.

…Church helped

Some women said that their faith played a vital role during this time.

I am also a woman of faith and I attend my local church every Sunday. It is like a second family to me. They are many mothers of all ages there. Older mothers and grandmothers can sense when something is not right. One day I went to church but I was a bit concerned about my daughter. At the end of the service, a lady who is in her seventies, so a grandmother signalled me to go to her. As soon as she started speaking, she knew exactly why I was concerned and told me what to do. I didn't utter a word, yet she could tell that something wasn't quite right.

…Chose to be quiet

Some mothers reported that they felt ashamed to talk about it. This made it worse for them. They didn't want to be perceived as incompetent parents. They viewed others around them as better mothers than they were. The mothers in their circle seemed to be doing their own thing and no one really initiated the conversation. As a result they chose to close up.

I sincerely believe that talking about issues can have tremendous benefits, so if you are a new mother and fall into this category. I would suggest that you find other new mothers different from the ones you are close to. You can't keep things in all the time, there is only so much that your heart can take at a time. Building up things is like a fizzy drink in a bottle. It stays still but the more you shake it, the more carbon dioxide bubbles are formed. The more shaking you do the more carbon dioxide builds up, and when you open it, it doesn't come out in an orderly manner but messes up the entire place. Conversely if you were to open the same drink when you are not rushing, it will come out nicely as you will be the one controlling the flow. Please control your flow by opening up a little and get the help you require.

…Sought professional help

Some of the mothers I spoke to sought professional help to deal with the issue. This category of mothers found it very hard to return to work after a long time off. They found that many things had changed in their work place. There were new policies and procedures in place. Their entire situation affected their confidence at work. They just did not know how to be an employee again. As we have discussed before. They decided to speak to counsellors and therapists who helped tremendously.

Others mothers consulted career coaches to give them a sense of direction. They were being helped to explore other possible professions. As a result, they were able to focus on the jobs or careers that gave them a sense of meaning but most importantly where they could easily incorporate their family live as well.

5. How did you get back on track?

...Acknowledgement
It is said that the first cure to anything in life is acknowledgment. When you acknowledge there is a potential issue, you are more willing to seek help and accept the prescribed remedy.

Most of the women agreed with me that we had to acknowledge that we were losing our sense of self after becoming mothers. We had to decide to conquer it, doing whatever it takes.

...Faith
Some women practised meditation, which helped sharpen their minds, relieve stress and anxiety. They also practiced Yoga which helped improve balance, endurance, flexibility and strength in their lives.

Most women said that their faith played a big role in their lives. When things got out of hands, they relied on their faith.

Personally, I am a Christian. Whenever I am faced with any confusion, dilemma or feel lost at any point in my life, I have my faith to fall back on. I believe I have God who I consider my father. I believe that when I talk to him through prayer, he will always come to my rescue.

…Exercise
Some mothers started to invest in their fitness. They joined or re-joined the gym. They embraced physical activities. They started to work on themselves and as a result they felt good about themselves.

…Accepting the situation
Most of the women I spoke with said that they had accepted their fate. They had to come to terms with their new lifestyle. They expressed that deep down they knew from within that they wanted to become mothers at some point in life. They therefore deliberately avoided thinking about the issue of loss of self-identity altogether. They decided to move on with their lives. I couldn't agree more with them on that. They also said that they have learnt to live with the situation and have adapted accordingly. They realised that it was a time to shift.

…Taking up a hobby
Some women decided to keep themselves busy by taking up a hobby. While on maternity leave, I kept myself busy, I developed an interest in candle making. I invested in the equipment and spent my time on YouTube learning how to make candles. I felt so good! I wasn't just a mother and a milk factory but I had something else to keep my mind occupied.

It is amazing how a small tweak in our routine can make a massive difference. I believe that whenever we are faced with anything difficult in life, we have to move our focus from the problem and think about solutions. Taking up this new hobby took my mind off certain motherhood dramas and helped me focus on myself. I will be touching on this later in the book.

...Further education
Some mothers said they started investing in themselves academically. They took it as a chance for a fresh start; they took on a course or went back to university to further their education.

...Coaches
There were other mothers who even consulted mind-set coaches. They felt they need to be helped with the way they thought about and viewed the world around them and just wanted professional help to navigate that journey. They claimed that it was a game changer and felt more in control of their lives.

It is worth mentioning that, there is not one practical book or formula to successful motherhood. The journey can be very bumpy but I really made peace with it. Whenever there is a conflict with my other responsibilities, I just pause. To be honest every aspect of my life is equally important to me and I have learnt to prioritise and choose my battles. For example, when I am working, I am not a mother but an employee. When I am a mother, I am not an employee. I am one or the other depending on the context. I have imaginary switch buttons in my brain; they are turned ON or OFF when needed. I have normalised my new life.

I appreciate that like anything, things do not always go according to plan, for instance when I am working remotely, my daughter is sometimes around. I can't just ignore her presence if she needs me. What I tend to do is, when in this situation, I take regular breaks so she feels I am also giving her some attention. Then I work longer to compensate for my breaks. I have a daily target with my job, so I endeavour to meet it before the day ends. Likewise, if I am working from the office and the nursery calls, I will have to drop whatever I am doing and pick it up again when able. These are very rare scenarios, though we have to expect the best and we have to prepare for the worse.

When you are busy working, you look forward to the weekends and your days off. Now that you have become a mother, whether it is the weekend or a day off, you have a permanent job pending at home. So, if you are still on maternity leave, I would suggest that you forget about work completely. Focus on the new assignment you have been given- in this case a baby. Just remember that feeling out of sync for the first few months is completely expected. Your routine will be all over the place. At the same time, you are picking up on things and learning the habits of your new baby. You will know when they sleep, eat, need changing and much else besides. You will become better at it. Once you are familiar with those, you can then use the time your baby is busy sleeping, to do something meaningful. Most of the time, you may get bored especially if you are consistently doing the same thing over and over – baby this, baby that I would suggest that you find something to keep yourself busy. Something else to look forward to. Learn a new language. Learn to cook. Take up a new hobby. Catch up on things you couldn't do because of your demanding job. I will be discussing this in more detail later in the book.

How does one know that self-identity is being lost?

Following up from the mothers in the survey, we found losing your identity can be a gradual process which can happen over time; it can happen over months or years but in some cases, it can happen suddenly following a major life event such as becoming a mother. When self-identity is lost, it can create a gap or a void.

I would like to share some pointers to look for to detect self-identity crisis:

...Not fitting in at work
When you return to work after your maternity leave, many changes may have taken place during your absence. It may be overwhelming to re-adapt. If this resonates with you, it may be that you built your identity around your competence and intelligence. When these foundations are shaken you can feel like you don't belong to your place of work anymore.

...Loss of passion
When you lose your sense of self identity, it can result in losing passion in the things you once deemed valuable. You cut ties completely with the things you used to enjoy doing. There can be a decrease in activities you found pleasurable before. You may disengage in the things that made you happy and gave you a sense of purpose.

...Loss of confidence
Losing your self-identity can make you lose confidence in your domestic life. You can also lose confidence at work. You may start underperforming. Your sense of value and self-worth can become dependent on external factors such as your physical appearance, success or status.

...Self-doubt
You may become extremely anxious and fearful about life. You may dread the idea of trying new things. You may even question your work ethics.

...Loneliness
You may start having social anxiety and become isolated. You may experience loneliness. You might prefer to be alone to avoid being talked to, which you can see as a threat when feeling like this. You can even think no one understand you or cares. All of which can threaten your ability to connect with others.

...Becoming vulnerable
When you lose your sense of self, you become vulnerable. You can start to seek validation or self-worth from other people. You start caring more how others view you. This is of concern as it causes you to seek reassurance and praise from other people so you can feel good about yourself. This does not eventually work, since our emotional well-being depends on how we feel about ourselves, not how others feel about us.

...Seeking validation
When your identity is dictated by others, it becomes an issue worth investigating. You should not be concerned about what others think about you, how you look, how you dress or carry yourself, yet you worry about being judged by others. However depending on external validation can prevent you from releasing the "real you". This can impact your personal growth and you not taking up wonderful opportunities that may come your way.

...Camouflage
This is when you pretend to be someone you are not. You pretend to be alright when you are suffering inside. You camouflage yourself, you put on a mask. You present your pretend best self to the world, whereas in reality you are a mess and finding it difficult to function. You can't keep on pretending.

Is identity loss a matter of perception?

Do motherhood experiences cause us to overcomplicate the role self-identity plays?

Please understand that I am not trying to undermine the seriousness of the issue but rather attempting to investigate possible causes in order to help us all.

Identity loss for working mothers is prevalent in our society today. As mothers, some of our jobs are contributing to our loss of identity in motherhood as not enough support is available. This has been supported by the survey results that we have discussed in details already. The question now is, is loss of identity subconsciously learned or perceived?

During my research I came across something called Accelerated Resolution Therapy (ART). It is essentially a form of therapy, which targets unresolved emotions and experiences. These unresolved emotions and experiences are stored differently in our memory. During the day, the brain processes any information we are exposed to. At night however, information is processed in the cerebral cortex. This is the outer surface of the brain, associated with consciousness, thought, emotion, reasoning, language and memory. There are three types of memory, sensual, short-term, and long term. These unresolved emotions and experiences stay below in the cerebral cortex. They free float like particles. This includes every aspect related to our survival. For instance, whenever we are faced with a potential danger, our brain recalls information from our memory in order to react.

I'd like to point out this therapy does not target symptoms but events. It reconditions stressful memories by changing how they are stored in the brain to improve mental health. It also reduces traumatic or stress inducing memories, it can also strengthen our resilience.

As we have seen, some mothers have experienced postnatal depression and postnatal anxiety. As ART consists of image re-scripting or image replacement, it changes feelings associated with past traumatic memories. It replaces bad memories with better ones. Affected mothers can look at their identity and see that motherhood is an additional facet of them rather than a replacement identity. Whenever the trauma is recalled from memory, it will no longer produce the same physical or emotional response

I really like this Approach and personally it gives me a sense of peace and normalcy. Please working mothers, I really hope you can reconcile the two. You need to learn to separate the ideas in your head. Your identity is you and being a mother is an addition or another identity that you possess. The former isn't there to replace the old but to work alongside it. It is vital to go on making an effort in both roles. When you are able to, do what makes you happy, have some "ME" time. This ME time doesn't need to be long just an activity which doesn't require you to be physically with your baby. Go have a pedicure or manicure, go for a walk in the park. Go to get some coffee and sit awhile. Pick up a book for an hour or so and read. Go for a drive. You know what makes you tick. You can be alone or if you prefer be with your friends given that your baby is not around. You can start to regain a sense of self-identity again.

If this idea doesn't do it for you, maybe take a shorter maternity leave. Work for me is the greatest distraction. So, if this rapidly restores some idea of self-identity, I would suggest you go back to work sooner. Maybe having that extra commitment, going to work, socialising with colleagues can accelerate that process. Once again do what works for you.

So that when your mothering duties call, you can give them your undivided attention, be there fully. Don't transfer your frustration to your child. They didn't ask to be born; you brought them into the world. So, please be the best mother you can be.

There is a saying; one can only give what you have. Unless you are happy with yourself, you can't transfer happiness to your child.

Ultimately you make the choice to be a mother or yourself and a mother as well.

Depending on your circumstances, if taking a longer time off work and solely focusing on your family helps, by all means stay at home. I appreciate that there are some stereotypes associated with stay-at-home mums. It is perfectly fine to take a career break to focus on your family. You have to do what works for you. People tend to criticise what they don't understand. Please know if you chose this, it does not make you lazy, un-ambitious and less driven. It is a temporary situation. You know where you want to go as a family. You have to close your ears to the noise of people outside. People take career sabbaticals, which is completely normal. Why should you feel any different?

I would suggest that working mothers who feel like they have lost themselves should make time for themselves while incorporating their children into their new identities. They might want to introduce boundaries which would help them differentiate between being a mother at home and an employee at work.

I wanted to mention the study below which was investigating how both working and non-working mothers cope with stress. I was intrigued by the fact that in both cases stress is involved.

A study by Ridhi et al. (2020), investigating parenting stress and coping strategies adopted among working and non-working mothers and its association with socio-demographic variables:

This cross-sectional study was carried out in India, and their results showed that 13% of non-working women and 26% of working women experienced high levels of stress. Further, a significant proportion of working mothers had parenting stress which necessitated interventions in the form of promoting mental health and providing crèche facilities at work.

These results suggest that motherhood can be very stressful, whether you are working or not. It is obvious that our careers can increase our stress levels. In these cases, I am assuming their work places invested in creche facilities. Sadly, this is highly unlikely to happen in the United Kingdom, where you are expected to separate your personal life from work.

It is also important to highlight that certain stresses in motherhood can depend on the health of the child. When there are concerns over a child, it can fundamentally shake a woman's self-identity. A friend of mine was affected in this way. Her son was diagnosed with Autism and her self-identity was shaken to its core affecting her mental health. She kept blaming herself. She believed that it is entirely her fault.

Woman's sense of identity can be transformed during the transition into motherhood.

Though we are living in a modern liberal democracy, in some parts of the world women are still not permitted to work in certain fields or professions. As we have seen earlier, in parts of the Middle East, including Saudi Arabia, this is still the case today. If for women going out alone is still heavily regulated, how much more so the world of work? I wonder whether these women view marriage and starting a family in the same as we do. I wonder whether their self-identity is challenged in motherhood much like ours? I can only assume that motherhood in their case, will be an imposed identity but at the same time, a form of self-identity. If this were the case, would it be fair to suggest that perhaps women in the West suffer loss of identity because they see their careers as their identity.

I wanted to highlight another study supporting working mothers.

A very recent study by *Emily et al. (2022) on the bright side of motherhood – a mixed method enquiry.*

This study suggests that actually motherhood and coping strategies can enhance a woman's knowledge, skills and capacity. At the same time, it strengthens her mindset, willpower and overall emotional intelligence. These are desirable attributes in the workplace. Further, motherhood can unlock a woman's potential and prepare her for management and leadership.

I really hope that you are somehow comforted by the above study. We all know how motherhood is stigmatised in society. It is believed that it also negatively affects a woman's careers. The only thing I would add is that, research is one of the ways we can change the narrative concerning motherhood, however, it will require some courage and self-belief that we are able to deal with our dual responsibility and be the best we can at both.

Is Self Identity A Cultural Issue?

In most developing economies, including the one I come from, The Democratic Republic of Congo, historically it was a patriarchy where women depended on their partners or family for survival. Hence, having children was one of the means of investing in their future, the more children you had the better your chances of being looked after in your old age. I would also like to mention that for a woman who couldn't have children, it meant that she was subjected to mockery and shame, especially by her family as she wasn't considered marriage-worthy.

Age also played a major factor – the younger a woman was, the more fertile she was believed to be and the more likely to be given in marriage. This is one of the reasons women then had their children very young. I think of my grandmother. She was given to be married at 13 to a 60-year-old man. This meant she started giving birth as a teenager. Although this is an extreme example – the average age would have been no more than 16.

Our tradition still requires the man and his family to pay a dowry. Basically, no marriage is recognised until the latter had been paid to the woman's family and accepted. This exchange can be very costly as many factors are taken into consideration such as the woman's education – the more educated the woman, the higher the dowry price. Another factor they consider is if the woman is a virgin or hasn't had children outside of wedlock that also increases the dowry price. Since a dowry requires finances, many younger men aren't able to afford marriage. Therefore, the family opts for the best candidate who can afford marriage, unfortunately, they are often older men and some women won't accept marriage under these conditions. Consequently, they grow very high-powered careers and some men are intimidated to ask their hand in marriage.

One thing I remember is men tended to be polygamous. This then caused women to be more independent, growing their own produce, to insure that their children and families had food to eat. They also became very entrepreneurial; they were involved in microbusinesses in the community, where they could sell the excess produce from their fields such as cassava, yam, nuts and fruits. This was also a way of generating some money to have in case of an emergency. Women also had mutual funds or partner schemes – it is called *likelemba* in my native language. It is essentially a group of women coming together and deciding on how much they would each contribute to the fund and for how long. For example, ten women decide to each put £1,000.00 a month for ten months. The first person gets the money the first month and it goes around in turn until everyone has had their share. These women did not have jobs in the same way we see employment however they were hard working and innovative.

The 21st century woman has other priorities such as education and a career, the idea of having children is usually nowhere on her radar or she's decided to leave it for a bit later. This has caused a major shift in the society. Women are having children much later in life. It used to be popular to have children in your twenties but today women are having their children in their thirties and, even in their late forties.

Today in my country, though, most women are expected to become mothers, society also encourages women to become more independent and be able to stand on their own two feet. That's why you see even those who are highly educated or hold very prestigious positions in corporations or in government, being mothers. As a woman in that part of the world, you are seen as a mother before any other title is bestowed upon you. Also, because of the way society has been set up, it is very affordable to look after children. Either family members, the community or a paid nanny can do this. You will have help. Again, that's why you see women having as many children as she they want without their jobs or titles being affected.

In my family, every woman is pro-education and career driven. My grandmother who was not educated but was given in a forced arranged marriage to an older man – ensured that her children would be educated. She was very entrepreneurial. She had a strong business acumen. She was very good with money – she knew about investing and saving. She passed this knowledge to my mother, who was very educated and family driven. My mother had 5 children and that didn't stop her from working full time. Having these two strong women as role models has helped me immensely. Whenever I feel like giving up, I hear their voices echoing if they made it, I can too. It is in the blood! I wanted to introduce these very important women in my life to explain where I get my inspirations from. Also what has been a driving force behind my transition from womanhood to motherhood.

This is the story you will hear in most parts of my native country. Women are encouraged to take dual responsibility. I am glad to have witnessed this in my life. Though things can still be improved, in some areas, women can assume both roles of being a mother and working without restrictions. They can choose to handle both their careers and family without feeling any less of a person.

The same study that I've already mentioned by (Ridhi et all, from 2020), also confirmed that a large percentage of women in India work, for example in the software industry 30% of the workforce are women. In agriculture and allied industrial sector, it's 89.5%. Most of these women are also mothers. Again, this study highlights the importance of women in the workforce and their invaluable contributions to society today.

Now, in the west however, I have observed things to be slightly different. Most women feel pressured to choose whether to have a career or children. When a woman announces that she is pregnant, people are excited at first and then they start making comments or asking silly questions like, it is not easy or can you afford it. The worst is when they want to have more children, oh my God- it feels like an offence! Why do you want another one, some ask. If anyone asked me that, my response would be: why are you bothered? Mind your own business please.

As living costs and childcare are rising astronomically, fear is mounting. Most jobs are not family friendly – which then reinforces this fear. There is a sense of increased loss for many women, when it comes to promotion for instance, some employers prefer male candidates as they are less likely to be off work for a long time. As already discussed previously. To some, they assume that having a family or children may cause you not to be up to the task due to divided commitments. I therefore think that all these factors contribute to the way women who are either intending to have a family or have already started are viewed in our modern society.

As a woman and a mother, I think it is very unfortunate to be treated this way. The only thing I can tell you is, it is work, I mean hard work, extremely consuming work being a parent but at the same time, there is nothing in this world that brings me as much joy as my daughter. For this reason, I want other women who wish to have children to know that it is rewarding and nothing can be compared to it. The way I see it, anything in this life has challenges to some degree but that doesn't stop us from living or existing. Our jobs can wear us out as they can be very demanding at times but yet we are still working. When you are a certain age, no matter how much you love your job, you will be asked to retire. When you are a parent on the other hand, you can never retire from your role.

Please understand that I am not saying it is easy to start a family or have children but rather it should be a personal choice not the result of pressure from society, not because you fear being judged for not having them.

How Did Previous Generation Cope With Identity Loss?

Society tolerated or should I say was initially designed with motherhood in mind. There were of course issues of inequality and sexism but motherhood was sacred. A woman accepted her primary role of becoming a mother. When she became a mother, she was psychologically ready for the demands and changes expected in her new role. Also, the community played a major role. When a woman gave birth, she was surrounded by her community- where she was coached by the older mothers. The new mother was given a hot bath by an older mother, her own mother or from the community. She was taught how to look after herself and the baby. She was never alone and the baby was taken care of. For a few weeks, she was encouraged to rest as they believed when the body was relaxed, milk production accelerated. We now know that prolactin, the hormone responsible for milk production is enhanced if the mother is relaxed. They also believed, and we know it to be true, that breastmilk is very important for the baby's development and the mother's interaction and connection to her new baby.

My Personal Experience

I became a mother in my early thirties. I had no help and because of the pandemic no antenatal classes were being run. I had to learn things myself. Thank God for YouTube! As the senior member of my team I'm so accustomed to my role I can do it with my eyes closed! Here I was faced with a seemingly impossible task. What should I do? How do I know what she wants? I had my to-do list: milk, I've made sure she has burped, I've changed her nappy, I've put on clean clothes… What else does she want? What is wrong with her? Is she breathing? I laugh.

It wasn't easy but if you're willing to try, you can do it. Things start off complicated but with time, you get used to them. I remember not being able to sleep at all because I thought if I did, something would happen to her. I was so exhausted! However, the more time passed, the more I developed a routine. It's believed that if you repeat the same activity for a consecutive 21 days, it develops into a habit. You train your brain that way- I appreciate with a child, nothing is predictable. However, as promised, I'm going to list some tips which you can adopt to help you on your journey.

Before I start listing them, I just wanted to remind us all that our careers do not identify us! Our identity doesn't solely lie in our careers. This idea is false! Most of us trade our time for money and we aren't happy. Just consider how you feel on a Monday morning- how you always complain about how fast the weekend has gone? This alone is an indication that you are not happy with your job. After you have used up your maternity leave, don't go back to a job that brings you no purpose. It is vital to use this time when you are feeling lost or are on the verge of losing your identity as a new working mum to reflect on your life. Take yourself out for a coffee or lunch and have this conversation with yourself. Do it in a different environment away from your home so that you can detach a little from the emotional pull of a new baby and clear your mind. Remember I am not asking you to worry but to think instead! Bring a pen and paper or for the technology savvy bring your iPad or Note Books. Ideas are always floating in the air but only people with a clear mind are able to catch them.

We are multifaceted human beings- we are emotional, sensual, spiritual, relational, physiological and intellectual beings. We have to endeavour to cater for all our needs.

During this exercise, please do not think about anyone else, but look within yourself. The answers you will need have to be fetched from the inside of you.

Now, let's see some tips that can help you overcome this sense of losing yourself as a new working mother.

I appreciate that there is no formula or map to follow, however, I am going to be sharing some of my tips, I hope it will help.

Being a mum is part of you now and it will always be, however, it doesn't have to define you completely. You are far more than the role. I would suggest that you take some time and figure out how you want to define yourself. Here are a few pointers to help you:

- Now that you have become a mother, don't resist your new role and look for an escape. Please accept it and embrace it

more deeply. Do also accept your new child and try not to see them as an inconvenience.
- You have to work on your mind set from being stuck with your child to choosing to be with them. I appreciate that some days are longer and harder, but take heart.
- Change your mantra, from it is too hard to work and be a mother to I can make it work on my terms.
- You can't separate a mother from her child and vice versa. Without one, the other wouldn't exist. If you the mother lose yourself, your child will also lose themselves.
- As lovely as your child can be, please do not revolve your life around your child. Engage in other self-involving activities.
- Please don't stop caring about how you look. Just because you are a mother doesn't mean you can't look presentable. Fix your hair, put on your best lippy and wear your favourite perfume. Looking good can elevate your mood.
- Please do not revolve your life around your profession. Remember that's only one of your many facets. Get involved in things that align with your core values
- Please don't use validation and satisfaction of a job well done at work as the barometer of your self-identity.
- Please note, you have not lost your freedom but you have expanded into another dimension in your life.
- Please find new ways to connect with friends: instead of regular nights out, find alternatives, for example – have play dates or book clubs, instead of going to the cinema, plan an outing to the park or zoo. The idea is for you to still keep in touch with aspects of your former self.
- Please find a hobby – it can be a good idea to revisit the hobbies you used to enjoy before you became a mother. It will jog your memory and give you a sense of reconnecting.
- Please stop comparing your former and current situation. Learn to be content with each season and enjoy the ride.

We strive to be better than we were before or better than our mothers were. You'll find out that you'll fail over and over again. It is your battle and only you can fight it.
- Just remember, your new world is worthy of discovery. Meet new people. Make decisions that will propel you to where you need to be.
- Remember you've still got it, sometimes it is not courage we lack but information. Get informed so that you can make informed decisions.
- Please note you don't need to suffer in silence. Don't be ashamed to seek help, whether professional or from people close to you or even a stranger.
- Please take care of yourself, don't neglect things that used to bring you joy and pleasure.
- Please know that coming to terms with the fact you'll never have the life you had pre-baby takes time and that's ok. Your identity isn't lost but suppressed!

Here are some tips you can do on a personal level:

1. Take care of yourself
I know it sounds like a cliché, but when becoming mothers, we can easily let ourselves go. Please know that you are important and it is vital that you don't neglect yourself.

2. Set simple goals
Think about what you want your day to look like. Write it down in detail and follow it through.

3. Schedule some ME time
When you are by yourself, do what makes you happy, have some "ME" time. This "ME" time doesn't need to be long but just an

activity which doesn't require you to be physically with your baby. Go have a pedicure or manicure, go for a walk in the park. Go buy a coffee. Pick up a book for an hour or so and read. Go for a drive. You know what makes you tick.

4. Connect with spouse / partner or friends
It is always a good idea to spend some times with the people who know you best. These people knew you before you became a mother so they can steer you in the right direction or bring back memories of the person you were before the birth.

5. Do something you enjoy
You need to do something which reconnects you with the hobbies you once enjoyed.

6. Stop comparing yourself
You need to stop comparing your life to those around you. One of the ways you can avoid this is by taking stock of what you have and develop gratitude. I personally did this exercise daily, I wrote down 5 things I was grateful for that day. This definitely helped me.

7. Get extra help
It is okay to ask for help from friends and relatives if you want some time to yourself. You don't have to do everything yourself.

8. Prioritise priorities
It's a no brainer, you need to prioritise things. I usually put them in three categories. The things that are high priority. The things that can be done later. Finally, the things that are unimportant.

Here are also some general tips you can use:

1. Don't compare your work and your baby
Having a job as you know is more structured. You have a starting and finishing time. If you're lucky, you can take a break. As challenging and demanding as your job can be, at the end of the week or month, you will get paid. Now, when it comes to having a child, there is no such thing as a starting and finishing time. You definitely don't get paid financially but it is so rewarding. Therefore, it's unfair to compare roles as they are polar opposites.

2. Be aware of your new role
When you are a mother you become aware that your life has taken a new turning, in other words you have transitioned from a point of looking and worrying mostly about yourself to now doing it for another person, in this case, your baby. Babies are very dependent on their mothers. They can't do anything for themselves. Think about this as if you were starting a new job. Most of the time, you are full of excitement and high hopes. You are determined to excel and show your new employer that you were the right person for the role. Especially during your probation period, you give your very best and perform beyond what's required. You go out of your way to ensure that you pass your probation and that you stay permanently in the job. In some cases, your performance is so marked you become the centre of attention. We all know what happens then, you become, the one to watch. I would suggest that you treat your new role as a mother in the same way. Give it your best against all the odds. Be the mother that everyone looks to. Show them that you've got what it takes.

3. Acceptance
You need to accept that your life has taken a 180 degree turn. You have to accept that now you you've become a mother, you can't socialise or be spontaneous in the same way as you were before.

You have to accept that your baby is your number one priority. Everything and anything revolves now around them. You need to accept that life in and of itself revolves around change in the first place. Change is a constant in life so you can choose to adjust to life as it happens. You can learn to accommodate the changes to fit your identity. I would suggest being very organised. Plan your social life in such a way that facilitates your life changes. For instance, instead of going to the cinema in the evening, do it during the day when your child is either at nursery or with a childminder. Before you go out, make sure everything is in order at home. The food, the laundry basically your to do list has been done, so that when you get back you won't have to tackle that list, you'll be able to put your feet up and get on with the rest of your day.

4. Review your perspective

If you still want to live your life the same way you did before becoming a mum, then you are opening the door to frustration. You have to look at things from another angle. You have to accept the change and stick with it. I would suggest that you don't judge things the way you did beforehand. For instance, prioritise priorities. What I mean is, live your life in such a way that you balance life and work. Work when it is time to work and leave work behind when you are at home with your baby.

5. Consider widening your friendships

Befriend both new and more experienced mothers. You will find that most issues are common when it comes to children, so you are more likely to get the right advice and be able to rely on their experience and learn from each other. Even when you are experiencing real difficulty, you can share ideas. You can also develop strong trusting relationships where you share babysitting duties giving each other much needed space, and your children friends to play with, which is great for their cognitive and social developments.

6. Get partner involved
If you are in a relationship, get your partner involved in the process. They may not fully understand what you are going through but sometimes the mere fact of having someone you can talk to and who listens to you, can make a tremendous difference.

Here some tips for your personal development:

1. Assess your current life
It's vital to be in tune with yourself by identifying your needs. What do you actually need to feel fulfilled? What needs to be changed in your life at this very present moment? What does the life you dream about look like? You have to work backwards. You must imagine what the ideal you would look like. It is just like driving. You type in your destination post code. The Sat-Nav will take you there. Your brain is also a navigation system. Fill it with images reflecting the life you want. Some call it the law of attraction. Whatever, you call it, it is fine as long as you are creating the images you want to bring to life. You must think about what the end result would look like then devise the strategies to get there.

2. Reconnect with your core values
What is the most important thing in your life? Core values differ from one individual to another. Core values are things like discipline, diligence, integrity, and accountability to name a few. I try to live by these core values. I believe that when my life is disciplined, I am able to obey rules even when I am tempted to deviate from them. I need diligence to see my dreams fulfilled without giving up. I need integrity as it describes who I am, my ethics and values. Finally, I need to be accountable for every choices and actions I take without blaming anyone.

3. Identify and eliminate any mental blocks

Identify and eliminate any mental blocks, internal challenges and limiting beliefs. These are assumptions that we hold to be true about ourselves, the world and reality. Unfortunately, these only hold us back and cause us to focus on negativity. They are often hidden but can affect us physically or mentally. These beliefs, mentioned earlier, originate from our lived experience and events. It's like the hard drive in a computer where memory is stored. They subconsciously internalise fear or insecurities, which translate into behaviours and the choices we make. The sad thing is they are often hidden and lie below the surface. They can also be very difficult to identify as they are ingrained within us. If they are unresolved, they can inhibit our progress. Examples of limiting beliefs can be lack of passion, low energy, or feeling lethargic about life in general.

4. Avoid third party approval and people pleasing

It's so common and saddening how we waste energy and efforts on people who don't matter! Everyone experiences challenge one way or the other – and comparing ourselves to them is an utter waste of time. Focus on your life, live as if nobody's watching. We are constantly burdened by what others think, who cares? These are the things which can contribute to internal conflict causing us to lose confidence in our lives. It gives us the feeling of not being enough. I always think of race horses. I don't know how knowledgeable you are about them. I learned that during a horse race some horses wear blinkers which limits their vision; they are generally used to help the horse concentrate on running and to reduce distraction. Thus, I suggest that you put your blinkers on ladies. Put them on so you can focus on priorities and minimise distractions. Comparing your life to others is a distraction. You don't have to respond to every barking dog you meet on the street, you have got things to do and places to go. Your time is precious, please use it wisely.

5. Mitigate limiting beliefs with affirmations

We tend to judge ourselves harshly at times. I personally think we find it quite normal to judge ourselves but when we are judged by others, we take it personally. It goes to show that we react to the truth. We just defend ourselves by getting angry. When you look at yourself in the mirror, do you like the reflection of the person you see looking back at you? Whether you like the image you see or not, try to change the narrative. When you look at yourself this time, see and say what you'd love to see. Speak good things about yourself. Use affirmations, even though you might not believe them. The more you practice this, the more confident you will become and the more natural it will sound. Eventually you will believe it. Tell yourself "I am Beautiful ", "I am the best mother", "I am a role model and people look up to me", "I am successful in everything I do", "I am the best employee an employer can ever have" – use personal pronouns, "I am" statements and add anything you want.

6. Rekindle the passion in your life

What makes you happy? What are you passionate about? What brings you a smile? What can you do for the rest of your life even if you weren't paid? When we are passionate about something, it shows. People around us can attest to it. Passion can't be hidden. Therefore, when we are truly passionate about something, we are more likely to plan. Planning in itself helps you not to live on autopilot and just let life happen to you. But rather, it enables you to take control of your life. It also suggests that we believe in a better life or success. It provokes you to reach for your goals.

7. Form a clearer and realistic vision for your life

You know where you are but do you know where you are going? Do you know what it will take to reach there? When cooking, we follow a recipe- if you are baking a cake for instance, you have a set of ingredients which are essential to make that cake look like one on the recipe. You need butter, eggs and sugar. Each step you take matters to bake a successful cake. If something like a cake needs a road map, don't you think your life, which is far more important, needs one too? Determine where you are going and take corresponding actions towards your goal until they materialise.

8. Formulate an action plan

Create a vision board. If you are not familiar with a vision board, it is simply a board where you record all your dreams. It is believed that when your eyes keep seeing the things you want, your subconscious will attract them, it's the the law of attraction. You attract what you see frequently. So put your vision board where you are most likely to see it on a daily basis. Think of a place in your house that you definitely go to often. One of the great places people tend to put them is on the fridge. You always use your fridge so as you are opening it, you are reminded of your vision. Or you can use the bathroom like I do. I use my bathroom often and my vision board is placed just on top of the basin. Every time I either brush my teeth or wash my hands, I look at it. You can put pictures on it, or words, all your dreams and aspirations. Then tick them off as you go along. So when one of the dreams comes to pass, tick the box or highlight it as done.

9. Motivate yourself

Motivate yourself to stay committed to keep track of your progress. You have to be your own biggest fan and cheerleader. Life is made of ups and downs. I personally live by this: expect the best and prepare for the worse. Regardless of the outcome, choose to stay motivated! Motivation gives you the courage and boldness to carry on especially when things get tougher. It will remind you of the reason you are doing whatever that is.

10. Find a mentor

Yes!- while there are so many misunderstandings when it comes to having mentors, it is very important to have one, especially in an area that we are still new to. When walking along an unfamiliar path, it is very wise to have a tour guide. Mentors are like tour guides. Every time I have travelled to a new country, I have had a tour guide or have hopped on a sightseeing tourists bus, I have learned invaluable historical information about a place in a short period of time, instead of me having to figure out things on my own, I often prefer having an expert guide me. The same principle could be extended to motherhood. Any challenge that you can possibly face, someone else has been there and conquered it. I would suggest that you be mentored by such an individual, it will make your life much easier. Just think about this, a mentor will practically show you how to do it. They watch you do it. They do it with you. Then, they leave you to do it alone, because you've learned how to do it and now you know what to do.

To benefit from your mentor, you have to be accountable and coachable. Remember you are the student and they are the teachers. This means when you are given a task to do, follow the instructions. Also, be open minded as your mentor could be younger than you. For everyone to benefit, there needs to be mutual agreement that age is irrelevant.

Once you are able to do the above, you will know your purpose. Most importantly, you will be able to find that work-life balance.

11. Look after your mental health

I'm sure you know how detrimental poor mental health can be. There are so many people in our generation who have been diagnosed with mental health issues due to the pressure of life. You only live once. We are all different – a challenge can seem insurmountable for some and for others, is of little concern. We have mentioned before that we shouldn't bow to peer pressure or comparing ourselves with others. If you can't manage work and being a mum, by all means, stop working. This doesn't make you incompetent or lazy. If your mental health demands that you take things slowly, stop. The child will grow. The skills you have you'll still have. Just because you have left the job doesn't mean you have lost your identity.

It is very important to highlight that work and motherhood do not define you. You are more than just these roles. You are made of gifts and talents that this world is waiting to discover. Cultivate those streams within you and allow them to flow out. They weren't meant to be contained. If you have already identified your gifts and talents, I am very happy for you. The only thing I would ask you to do is to sharpen them. Raw talent isn't enough. To be amazing you need to add skills to it. Once you have worked on them, they could be another source of income for you.

In Hindsight

I Personally, don't think I was prepared in any way when I first found out that I was pregnant. I had already been married for 4 years, all my focus was on my self-development, advancing my career and planning for the future, mostly financially. If I were to go back in time, I would tell myself to plan properly. To set specific, measurable, achievable, relevant, and time bound goals – following the SMART model. These goals would have kept me laser-focused on one thing at a time and be accountable as to when I needed it to be done. I would have to be honest with myself and know how far I could stretch. I understand that planning for a child doesn't always go to plan. I remember at one point I was actually planning for it but it didn't happen. I then relegated the idea and focused on other ventures. Pregnancy took me by surprise, it happened when we were least expecting it. I would definitely plan ahead financially. We all know how much money is involved in the process. I would budget properly in order to reduce unnecessary stress. I would prepare mentally especially with the changes involved. I am not talking about morning sickness but more in my marriage and social life. I would use the experience to bond more with my husband, not just when I felt the kicks and movements in my tummy but to also allow him to be part of the process. I would not over spend on things that weren't needed just because I was excited about having a baby. I would be more selective when it comes to advice and not allow every comment from other mothers to get to me. I would not doubt myself and the great job I was doing. I would trust my gut over certain things and not only rely on others. I would spend more time on maternity leave and witness all the development milestones my daughter has undergone.

Work-wise, I would ensure that the role I was applying for was flexible. I would go further in investigating the organisation's actual policies supporting parents.

Those are the things I could have done differently had I known certain things I know today. Expecting a baby is already very stressful on its own so reducing certain other stresses would have been ideal.

Why is Motherhood Important?

There is a war against women in modern society. Everything is designed to attack and destroy women. At the same time, women are the only humans able to reproduce. Without mothers, our society would become extinct. It is worth mentioning there is sufficient scientific evidence suggesting that many societies today are either having smaller families or are refraining from having children all together, suggesting that if this trend continues will time certain ethnic groups will disappear completely. We don't unfortunately have the ability to live forever. The only natural way to be replaced by the next generation is through childbirth. Conversely, certain ethnic groups today are still family driven and are still having a lot of children. I know of this friend who chose her career over having children. She was born from a family of two. After a few years, her parents passed on and she was only left with one sibling. This sibling only had one child, unfortunately, he passed on also. Now, this friend only has one living relative, and neither of them is family driven. To be honest, I am saddened by this, I appreciate that it is a personal choice, but the fact remains, when they both passed on, there is no generation to follow.

Certain realities in life can't be changed nor challenged. Mothers can't be replaced in society at least not as far as reproduction is concerned. This reminds me of the 2015 movie Selfless the story of a business tycoon and billionaire named Damian Hale. He is diagnosed with a terminal illness however, he doesn't want to die and as he is fabulously wealthy, a doctor Professor Albright helps him to save his life by transferring Hale's consciousness into a new, younger body. Well, later on in the movie, things don't go according to plan and the whole experiment fails.

What I am trying to say is certain things are just unnatural and if we attempt to fight nature, things can go disastrously wrong.

Naturally people belong to families. A society without a family has no boundaries. This is where mothers are needed more than ever. Mothers play a critical role in the family, which enables social cohesion and integration. Mothers are the bedrock of society. Mothers are naturally loving and caring. They are also nurturing and caregivers, this is vital for the healthy development of our children.

I really want to emphasise that mothers naturally exemplify unconditional love. From the time I conceived my daughter to the day she was born, everything in me screamed love. I loved her without knowing her. The nine months she spent in my tummy was just by love and through love. It required lots of sacrifices from me. I became selfless. It wasn't about me only her. I can tell you, that through her I understood what true love is. This love accrues the older she gets. I believe this was the kind of love my mother had shown me and I could feel it. This struggling society really needs motherly love.

I can't help but comment on the gang violence and selfishness in our modern society. People have become extremely greedy and so consumed by self that they ignore what is happening. One may call it itself love, but I respectfully disagree. We need love back in our society. This can only be restored when our modern society acknowledges the vital role mothers play and make the necessary efforts to value them again. They need to be rewarded as in doing so, we enhance our living conditions and securing a better future for all.

We can all agree that although the world is constantly changing one factor remains constant and that is that mothers are invaluable to society. Their importance can't be stressed enough, or their invaluable contribution to raising the next generation.

Is work necessary?
Society is held together by work. Work is the best distraction for human kind. In the same way, our physical bodies have to be taken care of, our minds also need to be maintained. Work is definitely paramount.

As working mothers, we are moulding the next generation and people around us by our activities. Experience is the best teacher people say. We learn through observation. So, as discussed previously, you are more than just a mother. You have so much potential which has to be unleashed to benefit the world. Not working prevents others from benefiting from your contribution and you from developing into the best version of yourself. Just like in spring, the trees shake off their old leaves to signify a new season, so are you with your life.

Legacy
Having a daughter has caused me to think about legacy. Even as a toddler I can see her mirroring what I do. I am her first role model. Any insecurity or issues, related to women, I will be her first reference point. Thinking about it puts pressure on me but it is a good kind of pressure. As I have learnt to overcome my own sense of loss of identity in motherhood, I feel equipped to pass on the baton if and when her time arises. I appreciate that the journey is still very long and there is always room for improvement.

My daughter is the force that catapults me to other realms. I want to be able to navigate these unchartered territories and conquer them so that my daughter can have a reference point when she in turn faces bias at work or loss of identity at any point in her life.

As women, mothers and professionals in our respective fields, let us endeavour to fight the status quo and fight for the injustices and insecurities we face daily. Let's work hard and pass on the baton to the next generation. As we discussed earlier, our predecessors fought for us to enjoy the freedom such working, voting and leading. Our sons and daughters are watching. They are observing and taking notes. They are the leaders of tomorrow. Our sons should understand that when they occupy positions of leadership in a government, organisations or companies, they should be able to accommodate working parents and give them the required support so that they can perform at work and look after their families. They should encourage a work / life balance. Our daughters should also learn from us that they can be anything they want to. They can occupy any desired position available in their profession. And if they choose to become mothers, they shouldn't fear to pursue their careers, ambitions, hopes and dreams because their mothers didn't.

It is said that educating a woman is education a nation. Women are powerful. We are able to convince, compel and revolutionise any institution. We should show our next generation that there is more to life than one's profession. They should know that they are humans first and foremost. A profession is just another facet of their life but not their identity. They should discover their core values and beliefs and from there develop their talents and gifts. They must then deploy them for the world's benefit. This is the only way we can all keep our identity without feeling trapped or lost. We all have a purpose bigger than our careers.

Finance

I found that most of the frustration in my motherhood journey was due to financial instability. This was echoed by most of the mothers I had spoken to. I would like you to do an exercise for me please. If you could shut your eyes right now, imagine your life if finance were not an issue. What do you see? Imagine that this was not a concern at all? When I did this exercise myself, all I saw was financial freedom and independence. I hope you saw something great too.

Admittedly, most of our pressures are financial, hence dependence on our jobs. In retrospect, when the pandemic was at its worst, many people lost their jobs and of course the welfare system couldn't support everyone. I don't know if you know of anyone who lost their jobs. I do, I knew many people in fact and the fear of the unknown was so pertinent. This is a very sad reality. Of course, when despair hits close to home, the natural reaction is to feel you could be next! When you have a family, the tension is even higher. The point I am trying to get across is that we should all endeavour to be financially independent. This is a must. When one is financially free, it reduces certain stresses.

When we get pregnant, after the obvious excitement, the next worry is, how are we going to cope financially? Before I became a mother, whenever I applied for a job, I was attracted by other incentives, maternity related issues were never on my radar. At that time, it didn't concern me and it wasn't relevant. To my surprise, when it became relevant, it was a different ball game altogether. I don't know how familiar you are with the support and incentives around maternity but they are very insignificant. Just in case you think that I am being ungrateful, I am not. I come from a country where people can only dream of what we get in the United Kingdom. I am humbled by the fact that it was available to me. I guess what I am saying is, endeavour to be financially independent. When you are financially independent, you decide on what matters to you most, to some it is having a family, or the number of children you would like to have if you want a big family.

So how does one become financially independent?

First of all, just like anything else, it is learnt. To drive a car, you need to do your theory test so that you know rules and regulation for driving on the road and are able to recognise different road signs and know what they mean. That's followed by the practical exam, where you are expected to put your theoretical knowledge into practice. The same rule applies to finance.

As a mother, it is very important that you are strong financially. What I mean is, you have to become a great accountant. Ensure that you account for all your income and expenses monthly or even daily. If you are very organised, it will be great to keep a spreadsheet. I recommend you know how much is going out in household bills. If you are renting a place, how much goes towards it. If you have a mortgage, how much is it? How much do you spend on food? How much on travel expenses? How much do you spend on your car? How much is allocated towards activities and socialising? These are just the basics.

You have to learn how money functions to know your liabilities and assets. Think about the future. Are you saving towards your children's future or are you just spending money carelessly and buying them the latest gadget in town? Do you have any financial goals for yourself? The rule of thumb is, your saving should amount to at least six months' worth of your wages. Basically, if the worse comes to worse, you should be able to maintain the same standard of living that you had for at least six months. Well, if you are already there, many congratulations, but don't stop there. There are at least three types of income one can have. The first one is your net income. This is your basic salary paid to you as a result of exchanging your time for money. You are paid because you offer a service, your current job.

The second type of income is passive income. Very self-explanatory, it is your extra income which is an increment to your already basic salary. Some people allocate this income to holidays, or retirement.

The last and less common is portfolio income. This is basically the money you receive from investments, dividends, interest, and capital gains.

Are you investing? I am sure you would agree that putting your money into your savings doesn't really increase due to a very low interest rate. You are more likely to see your money working when it is rightfully invested. One of the examples I could think of is property. It is bricks and mortar, durable and always needed as long as there are people. There are so many opportunities in property nowadays. There are so many strategies available that don't even require you to own your own property. I will list a few but this is just to encourage you to think bigger- to exercise your thinking muscles. Some of the common strategies are: Rent to Rent and Service Accommodation(SA).

Finance

Nowadays you can invest in many things, you can invest in your favourite supermarket. You can invest in real estate. You can buy stocks and shares. You can invest in Bitcoin or crypto currency. The list goes on.

I would suggest that you acquire a comprehensive understanding of money. Money is needed in everything so it plays an integral part in our lives but yet we don't seem to be interested in getting to know more about it.

We all have tremendous potential, and we all are blessed with gifts. Yet the one thing that holds all of us back is some degree of self-doubt. It is not so much the lack of technical information that holds us back, but more the lack of self-confidence. Some are more affected than others.

Let's explore our gifts ladies and work because we want to not because we depend on it. Let's gain our independence so that if we choose to become mothers, we'll be able to have as many children as we want because we are able to take care of them.

Let's also remember that problems are opportunities. Whenever there is a crisis, the number of millionaires increase. When faced with an identity crisis, look at it from a different perspective.

Let's become problem solver with our gifts. The talents and gifts we have were given to us in order to solve problems. You are the answer to a problem in this world. As long as we don't dive in and focus on them, nothing will happen. Let's create new narratives for our generation by providing solutions. Let's all discover, develop and deploy our gifts so we can live the lives we dream about.

Conclusion

We can conclude that it is very easy to lose ourselves in motherhood given the fact that it is very busy time with a never-ending list of demands. We are expected to look after everyone under our roof, they rely on us for everything such as cooking, and laundry and at the same time we have to look after ourselves. Now that we have become mothers, things are different. We are different now. We can't go back to our old self, we can only dream of the days when we took care only of ourselves. We watched what we wanted on television. Now, when making any decisions we consider another person our child. We put out needs and wants on the back burner in favour of our children. That's okay! This is our reality now.

As seen earlier, the brain undergoes neurological and structural changes causing it to redesign itself. It trims old connections and build new ones This suggest that motherhood will bring about certain changes in us inevitably. Most professionals tend to find the identity in their profession. This is not any different to working mothers. Since that sense of self-identity is built from work, when we become mothers it seems to affect us. We don't any longer feeling in control as motherhood is not structured. This collision of work identity and self-identity can be detrimental to our lives. It is important we redefine success regarding work. Let's extend some grace to ourselves by taking small steps, for instance, when you meet your target that day or month at work despite being a busy mother at home. It's a process of redefinition and transformation of self. As new mums we declare we won't give up our careers, sex lives, independence or identities just because we have a baby.

It is very important to know that our job is not the entire picture but rather one of our many facets. We have to accept that the women we were before becoming mothers is now a distant memory. That's okay.

We have to accept that changes have been incorporated in our lives, the things that made us unique don't exist anymore and we can even be unsure as to whether we will find them again.

We have to accept that our freedom is now restricted, we may not have enough hours to spare like before. That's okay.

Now that we have established and are accepting of the new identity that motherhood has bestowed upon us, we have to stop putting pressure on ourselves. Having a child is chaotic! You can't handle a child like you would do a job. You can't be rigid with a child. They are discovering the world around them.

We have to come to the realisation that our identity is not solely in our career nor is it in motherhood. We are first and foremost human beings. We are a treasure box filled with potential. We have to live for a purpose bigger that ourselves. We just need to be in- tune with ourselves.

We have to learn to ignore the seeming chaos around us. We have to focus on ourselves. I am talking to the real US. Our career has an expiry date. The current age for retirement at present is 67 years old. If we are only planning to invest in your career and nothing else, I think we would realise later on that we had nothing else to live for. Conversely if we'd given ourselves the opportunity to get to know ourselves, we would live a much more fulfilled life.

Dear mother, just know that you are very special. There is no one human being on this planet who is gifted like you are. I appreciate that peoples gifts can be similar, however there will always be a clear distinction. You and I can have similar gift but the way we unpack it will be different. For example, we can be both excellent singers, as closely related as this gift can be, our tone or ability to sing certain notes will differ. You are not competing with anyone else but yourself. Don't let your contemporaries advancement in life make you feel like you are delaying. Of course not. The aim is to be walking fully in your purpose.

I always believe in connectivity. There is a saying that you are one idea away from your dream. I can translate that to: you are one connection away from your dream. We need people, not necessarily those in our circle but also those who are very different from us. When we associate with dissimilar people we are exposed to different ideologies and ideas. It broadens our minds and the way we think. That being said, when we connect with other people, we learn and improve on ourselves. It is a transaction taking place.

On your journey to self- discovery in motherhood, many people will cross your path. You need to have an open mind and develop curiosity for learning. It is worth noting that not everyone is designed to stay with us all the way through but every single intersection serves a purpose. Look at the bigger picture and focus on your purpose. Some people will cross your path briefly but leave a mark that you will enable you to connect the dots to where you are going next. Others will stay for a long time or even a life time.

Your life resembles a tree. A tree is made up of many parts. It has roots. These roots are the foundation. They hold the pressure and sustain the tree. The trunk is the stem and main wooden axis of a tree. It is also the most important feature as it ensures that the entire tree is stable. The branches can be cut off. They can be cut off but the life of the tree is dependent on the roots. You have to become resilient in life especially as a mother so that you can develop strong roots to help you have a firm foundation. When the winds and storms of life arise, you will know what to do to survive.

As career driven myself, I would say, my career does not equate to my life. We stress so much about work that it feels at times like that's all there is in this life. Well, it is definitely not. No matter how good your performance, you are dispensable. I came across a post on LinkedIn where someone posted a similar question, basically whether it was fair for an organisation to view their employees as dispensable. There were divided opinions. The consensus held that it shouldn't be the case and they gave several reasons. Then a gentleman brought up a very interesting perspective. He said that a certain company had a very reliable CEO, who represented them well and displayed all the desirable attributes one CEO could possess. There was a plane crash and unfortunately, the CEO was one of the victims, he died. The company was affected and the people very saddened by the tragic news but after a month, the CEO was replaced. The company must go on! He concluded no one therefore is exempt. You can be made redundant or you can retire, either way you will be replaced and the show will go on. I don't know about you but this is just so true on many levels. So dear professional mothers don't neglect your family at the expense of your job. You won't work for your entire life but your family doesn't have an expiry date!

Final Words

Dear mothers, I am grateful that you have taken your time to read to the end of this book. I would like to leave you with this. The most important relationship you will ever have is with yourself. Your emotional well-being is dependent on how you feel about you as a result of the relationship you have within yourself. You have to be aware that you have lost your self-identity, as this is the first step towards finding yourself again. Once you are aware, you will have the opportunity to redefine yourself, explore who you are and what has made you into you. You will then find your own qualities and attributes and will no longer depend on external validation of others – it will in turn cause you to lose labels you have associated with yourself and pursue you true self.

I hope you have come to the realisation that self-identity is never lost but rather suppressed. You have always had it but just like anything else it can be submerged by others responsibilities surrounding your life. This can be a phase, it can come and go. If you feel like you have lost yourself on this journey – just know that you haven't lost yourself. You just need to reconnect. You have always had the power yourself. You just need to learn it. Just remember that having your first child and working is not easy but you have to fight against identity loss. If you don't you will lose your joy and block any sense of creativity within yourself. Go through this journey knowing how to maintain yourself in the midst of everything.

Suppressing your feelings doesn't make you stronger but rather weak and vulnerable. The other day I was in the shower and I wanted to use a razor. I realised that there was only one left but it was broken. One part was the stick to the razor and the other the actual razor. Since I was desperate I still used it and it worked. It still did the job.

I have always admired people who have real plants in their homes. I decided to joined the club also by buying a couple of plant pots for my house. I have them in my bathroom and kitchen. I water them whenever I can to ensure that they are healthy and growing well. I always check they are positioned where they can get some sun which is also beneficial for them. I started noticing despite my efforts that the leaves were drying out and they looked dead. I was disappointed because it felt as if my efforts were not being appreciated. Then spring came, effortlessly my plants started to grow new leaves and flowers again. I told myself, this is a lesson. My plants never died, the conditions were favourable for their growth, however, the old leaves had to fall to leave room for the new. You could use this analogy and remind yourself that it may seem like you have lost yourself on this journey but you have still got it, just keep on watering yourself, look after yourself like I did with my plants, you will grow again. Your spring will come and you will blossom again. Remember you have never lost it, you've still got it. You can be anything you want to be. You may be broken, exhausted and feeling inadequate, but just know even in that state, you are still capable of smashing your job and being a great mother for your child. In the words of The Wizard of Oz: "You've always had the power my dear, you just had to learn it yourself."

You are more than just a mother!

You are valuable: you are a value adder, you have contributed to the growth of our society. You are adding value to this world through your gifts and talents. This world wouldn't be complete without your presence. This world needed you and counts on you. Do not underestimate yourself.

You are loved: you are your child's world. You are the definition of love. You represent safety and comfort. That's why whenever your child is hurt; they first come to you, mummy! You have shown them the meaning of love through your sacrifice, dedication and hard work. They will emulate this everywhere they find themselves, even if you are no longer around. Your memory will forever be of love.

You are needed: you are the engine in your home. You are a breadwinner and represent strength. No one can do the things you do. You work hard at work and at home, you make it seem very easy. You are shaping our world's future through your contribution.

You are ambitious: you are not a pushover. You are determined to explore all the avenues of the talents you carry. You are great at your job. You have understood that you are not just a mother but full of hopes and dreams too. You have dreams that need to be realised. You have a purpose to fulfil.

You are a visionary: you are setting the pace for the world to see. You are emerging like an eagle, ready to spread your wings and soar. You are determined to make it through despite the challenges and difficulties you encounter. You know what you want for yourself and you are a go-getter.

You are a trailblazer: you are showing the world how things are done. You are not letting the status quo stop you from becoming who you want. You understand that there is more to you than your job or your children. You are a living proof that life belongs to those who dare.

You are a giver of life: you have sacrificed yourself to give someone else the chance to be alive. You are not selfish, you are the epitome of what it is to be sacrificial.

You are celebrated: a day has been set aside around the globe to celebrate you mother. The world recognises your need and has accepted that you are worthy of being celebrated.

You are so gifted: you are more than you give yourself credit for. You are so organised and ensure that things don't fall out of place. You spot an issue and are willing to resolve it because that's who you are.

You are so important: without you, life will be discontinued. Your children are the next generation. You are shaping the leaders of tomorrow.

Lift up your head, keep your chin up and straighten your back like the queen that you are!

Acknowlegements

The idea of this book sprung up from the conversations I have had with various women in my life. I would like to thank everyone who had participated in the survey. I thank you for sharing your experiences.

This book would not have been possible without the input of Anne Mosley, who I call my angel. I am forever indebted to you. I thank you for believing in this project and for taking the time from your busy schedule and help me think beyond my imagination. Words truly can't express my gratitude for you. I appreciate you.

Special thanks to my dear friend Harpreet Kaur, thank you for your support and encouragements. They mean a lot.

A massive thank you to pastor Michael Johnson. Thank you sir for your continual support and encouragements.

A huge thank you to DSJ for designing the cover

References

https://www.sciencedirect.com/science/article/abs/pii/S0266613808000764

https://www.sciencedirect.com/science/article/pii/S2213398420301962

https://www.sciencedirect.com/science/article/abs/pii/S0160738322000019

https://www.mother.ly/life/harvard-study-working-mothers-good-for-girls/?amp=1

https://hbswk.hbs.edu/item/kids-of-working-moms-grow-into-happy-adults

Printed in Great Britain
by Amazon